Truths, Trust and Translation

Michael En (ed.)

Truths, Trust and Translation

A festschrift, love letter and thank you to Michèle Cooke

PETER LANG

Bern · Berlin · Bruxelles · New York · Oxford

Bibliographic Information published by the Deutsche Nationalbibliothek
The Deutsche Nationalbibliothek lists this publication in the Deutsche
Nationalbibliografie; detailed bibliographic data is available in the internet
at http://dnb.d-nb.de.

Library of Congress Cataloging-in-Publication Data
A CIP catalog record for this book has been applied for
at the Library of Congress

Cover:
Illustrations by Afishka (shutterstock.com); adapted by Michael En

The printing costs for this book were partly funded by the

Centre for Translation Studies, University of Vienna.

ISBN 978-3-631-82528-0 (Print)
E-ISBN 978-3-631-82849-6 (E-PDF)
E-ISBN 978-3-631-82850-2 (EPUB)
E-ISBN 978-3-631-82851-9 (MOBI)
DOI 10.3726/b17300

© Peter Lang AG, International Academic Publishers, Bern 2020
Wabernstrasse 40, CH-3007 Bern, Switzerland
bern@peterlang.com, www.peterlang.com

Contents

Michael En

Texts, teas and thank yous: An Einleitung

This is a love letter. A lovely letter. A lot of letters. A festschrift. A sanftschrift. A thank you. A Dankeschön. A Sammelband. A collection of truths. A bouquet of flowers and of more that has grown and blossomed. A bundle of lightning flashes. A translation of *oh so much, if only we knew how to tell you ...* dedicated to Michèle Cooke, philosopher, translator, cow aficionada, 'mother, father, friend and lover, teacher, student, child and sometime sage'[1].

This *Sammelband* contains (*versammelt?*) contributions (*Bänder?*) from some of Michèle's former students and a special guest, all of whom have added to this book in their own unique ways. Michèle has always encouraged her students and friends, also by great example, to walk new paths – be it a *bóthar* with the width of two cows or some other way along a *roter Faden* – and explore whatever our creativity can surprise us with, and this book is a reflection of this approach. As expressed in its title, I invite you to read the contributions in this book as attempts, inspired by Michèle, to find the *truths* in our realities, to gain *trust* in ourselves, and to discover (the) everything in *translation*.

Don't let yourself be intimidated into reading this book a certain way by the table of contents. Indeed, feel free to start, pause, continue and end where- and however you like.

If you do decide to follow the flow of the pages from here on, you will find next a special message from Alexander Kravchenko, who calls on us as languaging beings to make friends with what Michèle once analysed as the elephant in the translatory room and to go out of the room with it together, to find the elephant right outside the door.

In my contribution, I talk about bullet-points, poems and cows to reflect on some of the ideas that have structured my own journey towards truth, trust and translation on which Michèle has guided me from the very beginning.

Benjamin Schmid reflects on and creates 'the music in a name', translating 'Michèle' into song and offering us, as he calls his chapter here, his extended liner notes, including on music as translation.

Michaela Chiaki Ripplinger looks at, as Michèle has called it, 'the human factor' in relation to (new ways of) machine translation, pondering what might

---

1 'Me, Michèle' on michelecooke.com 2020.

happen to 'translation' if what we come to expect as potential source texts and best-case target texts is more and more defined by technology only.

Aurelia Batlogg-Windhager invites us to join her on her journey into the core of translation and the heart of human existence: connection. Her guides are memories, recipes and milk jugs. In the end, there's even cake – if we decide to make it.

Boka En muses on categorisation, recognition and the dangers of making things clear, between avocado toast, relationship research and the blurriness of understanding. We can add our own notes, too.

Rehana Mubarak-Aberer presents her own collection within this collection and tells stories. About death. About love. About goslings and bears and halibuts. Stories of what we find hard to talk about, to live with, to understand.

Daniela Schlager takes us along on a journey in a love(ly) letter about twist(ing), daring and *trainslation*. Take a seat, enjoy the scenery – and let yourself be moved.

One of the many joys of life Michèle appreciates and likes to share with others is *a good cuppa*. As someone who has often had the pleasure of being treated to this simple act of kindness by Michèle, I present each of the contributions in this book with its own tea recommendation, specifically chosen to fit the character and mood of the text as I experience it. Whether you see it as a reminder to put the kettle on more often or a potential starting point for kindling a new passion for hot leaf water, I hope these suggestions will add to an enjoyable reading experience. Should you end up experiencing the taste of a chapter in a very different way from what the contents of your cup suggest, I hope you will forgive me and savour the deliciousness of contrast.

In addition to the authors named explicitly in this book, there are also those who are present in it in other ways. Those who wanted to write something but couldn't. Those who didn't feel ready. Those who didn't feel right. Those too close; those too far away. And those who I am sure would have wanted to say-do something but didn't get the chance because I do not know (of) them and had no way of reaching out to them (I'm sorry). I like to think that all of them are still part of this book, that it can serve as a symbol of the courage and love that Michèle has inspired in all of us and in so many more. And maybe, hopefully, this book will serve as inspiration for you, dear reader. 'Let the way that we think-feel-see be the way that we write'[2] – and let the way that we write enrich the way that we think-feel-see.

---

2   'Beyond Boxes' on michelecooke.com 2020.

I would like to say thank you to everyone who contributed to making this book possible, in particular all the authors present here in name. Without them, this book would not exist. Special thanks go to two people who helped me shape this project and make it reality: Renate Resch, who has been there with me from the beginning, and Chuck Spitzl, whose presence outlasts any absence. Finally, I thank the *Zentrum für Translationswissenschaft*, in particular Hanna Risku and Gerhard Budin, as well as the authors for their financial support for this project.

Most importantly, this book – the stories in it and behind it, the love and the letters, the words and the spaces between them – is how we would like to say thank you, Michèle. Thank you, Michèle.

Vienna, spring 2020

Alexander Kravchenko

On elephants in linguistics

So let us acknowledge the elephant.
For ourselves, to acknowledge our own relation to what words do with us.
For others, to be aware that they seldom speak what they mean,
and that language is first and foremost a relational process.
And in our study of human communication, so that we don't forget that
it's not primarily about words, language, power or hierarchies.
It's about relating the unsayable
so that we can relate to each other.

The elephant in the room.
Communication, chaos and the translation of truth.

Tea recommendation for this chapter:
Chai, with a peanut-sized drop of milk or your favourite dairy-substitute drink.

Elephants are fascinating animals – no wonder they have been a source of many metaphors we use to speak about something big and unusual that unfailingly attracts our attention. In her wonderful essay *The Elephant in the Room*, Michèle Cooke (2016) gives a witty critique of Wissenschaft as an activity whose intended purpose is to study the 'objective' world and what happens in it in order to discover some universal truth, or truths, about this world. Once discovered, described and generalized, these truths become the guiding stars in our lives, which we must follow if we do not wish to go astray, blunder, or simply look foolish in the eyes of the academics as holders of the truth. Thus, 'objectivity' becomes synonymous with 'scientific', while 'subjectivity' is 'the four-letter word of Wissenschaft' (Cooke 2016:70). However, argues Cooke, to practice this kind of Wissenschaft – specifically, in regard to language as the object of study in linguistics, a self-defined science – is to turn a blind eye to the truth in the form of the elephant in the room whose presence is quite obvious and cannot be denied: the truth that we are unable to tell the truth, if the function of language is communication as exchange of information aka truths about the world.

I find the elephant-in-the-room metaphor more than appropriate in characterizing the stance taken by mainstream linguists both in academic and non-academic circles when they observe, describe, and generalize what they believe to be language as species-specific activity with a particular function, and I would like to extend this metaphor in a somewhat radical manner: The elephant in the room is a young animal; there is another, older elephant right outside the door, looking for his son. We can try and learn to live with the one in the room, even invite it to tea, but we cannot leave the room because of the clear and present danger posed by the old bull out there. Linguists who believe in the communicative function of language choose to pretend that there is nothing of interest outside the room, so why bother looking out or even try opening the door? But the old bull is there, and he will not leave. Are we prepared to spend the rest of our lives confined to the four walls of the room, oblivious of the wonderful great world out there? And what are the chances that the old elephant will not tire of waiting and decide to force the walls, bringing havoc and chaos? Would it not be wise to finally notice the elephant inside and let it go, eliminating the danger and getting the chance to see beyond the walls of the room?

Of course, to answer all these questions, we must understand what this other elephant is. And to do that, we must ask the one question about language that traditional mainstream linguistics has never asked: 'What is the biological function of language?' To the hardcore orthodox linguist, it would be rather odd to even play with the idea that language should have a biological function (I bracket out biolinguistics of the Chomskian brand with its idea of language organ as a mere curiosity – for a witty critique, see Everett 2005). Although a lot has been said and written about language functions over the past century, with the entrenchment of the code model of linguistic communication in mid-20th century, the core function of language has been viewed, largely, as message (information) transfer from sender to receiver. That such transfer – even assuming that something *is*, indeed, transferred in linguistic communication – is more often than not unreliable and imprecise, making understanding an endeavor that challenges our wits and brings frustration and disappointment, not to mention occasional disasters, is usually explained by the so-called 'extra-linguistic factors' and pragmatics as the study of ways in which context contributes to meaning.

Now, if linguistics is a 'real science' with a well-defined subject matter (language as a sign system, or a code, used in an instrumental function for the transfer of mental content and studied in itself and for itself – the infamous tenet of Saussurean structuralism), why on earth, in explaining the function of language as part of 'objective reality', would it appeal to something external to it, thus contradicting its initial maxim? As for linguistic pragmatics, which encompasses speech act theory, conversational implicature, talk in interaction and other approaches to linguistic behavior, it is typically seen as the service-tool of semantics and syntactics – the real dimensions of linguistic semiosis in structural linguistics – whose job is to help understand what exactly is trans-ferred – and how and why – in a particular instance of linguistic communication as exchange of information. However, this model is not particularly helpful in understanding the crucial difference between the linguistic communication of humans and non-linguistic communication of other animal species, if the pur-pose of communication is transfer of information. It would be silly to deny that wolves, monkeys, dolphins or what have you are capable of communicating in this sense (I do not even touch here upon the issue of information as a notion that has been much misused and abused in popular discourse, linguistics being no exception; for more detail, see Kravchenko & Payunena 2018).

The narrow and restrictive understanding of linguistic pragmatics (cf. Kravchenko 2011) underplays the role of the interpreter as a constitutive com-ponent of semiosis – the process in which something functions as a sign. A sign is always and only a sign to someone capable of interpreting it as such. If we compare the narrow understanding of linguistic pragmatics with the domain of pragmatics in the theory of signs developed by Morris (1938), we will see that, before discussing syntactics as the domain of relationships between linguistic signs, and semantics as the domain of relationships of signs to objects to which signs are applicable, linguists should have a clear understanding of the nature of relationships between the interpreter and what the interpreter perceives as signs. In other words, why and how does the interpreter decide that something *is* a sign of something? And, in general, of what use are signs, linguistic or other kinds, to their interpreters anyway? Until linguistics addresses these questions in a straightforward manner and answers them coherently and unequivocally, it will continue groping 'the elephant of language' like the notorious blind men of Hindustan from John Saxe's satirical poem, never having a chance to get the real picture of the animal. However, mainstream linguists are unwilling to part with Saussure's semiology, which holds that linguistic sign as an arbitrary pairing of form and meaning is the paradigm sign for the study of all other semiotic systems – a claim as much unjustified as it is logically unsound. Overlooking the fact that humans are a biological species, and whatever unique features they possess must be explained from the point of view of biology as 'the mother of all diversity' (Givón 2009), orthodox linguists worldwide continue to develop, elaborate, and offer – as better, refined, or even new truths – various theoretical frameworks for explaining the nature and function of language, pretending not to see the elephant in the room and totally failing to see the elephant outside.

But what *is* this other elephant of whose existence orthodox linguists seem to be unaware? Is it really there, or, perhaps, is it just a figment of someone's imagination? The answer is: Yes, it is there and everywhere, and there's no running away or hiding from it. It is *semiosis as a foundational principle of life* in general, and linguistic semiosis in particular as a basis on which our humanness rests – 'a difference which makes a difference' (Bateson 1972) in the world of the living. The realization by some biologists and semioticians that semiosis is the divide line between life and inanimate matter has led to the emergence of a new paradigm in the study of life processes – biosemiotics (cf. Sharov 1992), a transdisciplinary research paradigm that becomes more and more noticeable on the academic horizon, opening new exciting prospects for the life sciences. But mainstream linguistics, with its dehumanizing approach to language as something segregated from man as a living system, does not seem to be concerned at all about becoming a life science. It wants to continue to study language as something superficial, something that comes after sapience and, therefore, is secondary to it, rather than as a biologically central and perceptually salient feature of the species *Homo sapiens*. The code model of linguistic communication – the hallmark of mainstream linguistics – obscures the nature of linguistic semiosis as a biological adaptation, and linguistics will not come any closer to understanding its object of study until linguists learn to speak differently about language and see continuity between life and language (Di Paolo, Cuffari & De Jaegher 2018).

This continuity was pointed out by Morris (1938), who saw the response to things through the intermediacy of signs as a biological 'continuation of the same process in which the distance senses have taken precedence over the contact senses in the control of conduct in higher animal forms; such animals through sight, hearing, and smell are already responding to distant parts of the environment through certain properties of objects functioning as signs of other properties. This process of taking account of a constantly more remote environment is simply continued in the complex processes of semiosis made possible by language, the object taken account of no longer needing to be perceptually present' (Morris 1938:32). And as was very convincingly shown by Gibson (1979), perception is ecological by nature, that is, *relational*. The function of the senses is to help a living organism relate to its environment by orienting to what may be of value to the organism in terms of preserving and sustaining its unity as a living system. Thus, the function of language is also relational. Referring to *The Origin of Humanness in the Biology of Love* (Maturana & Verden-Zöller 2008), Cooke (2016) reminds us that language is 'the constitutive element of human relationing. [W]e do not *use* language as an instrument, but are formed as languaging beings' (63; original emphasis). We are linguistic organisms, and we exist as languaging beings in the relational domain of linguistic interactions with others and self.

The relational domain of languaging is what distinguishes the systemic (cognitive) behavior of human society as a living system from other living systems. What is essential, however, is that while this behavior depends on the cognitive properties of the system components (individual languaging humans), these cognitive properties *emerge* in the domain of languaging as systemic behavior that becomes a cognitive niche for human organisms constructed by these organisms (cf. Sinha 2015). This crucial circumstance highlights the ecological nature of the relationship between human society and its domain of linguistic interactions. As argued by Maturana (1970:4), 'the evolution of the living systems is the evolution of the niches of the units of interactions defined by their self-referring circular organization, hence, the evolution of the cognitive domains'. Therefore, ignoring the ecology of language as a relational (cognitive) domain obscures our understanding of the processes that shape both individual and social cognition. Thus, the elephant outdoors becomes invisible – but no less dangerous. And what *is* the danger?

The danger is of the same or even higher order as in the case of global-scale ecological disasters brought about by messing with Mother Nature. Messing with language, trying to change it based on often misconceived ideas of the nature of human sapience and the function of language, is fraught with disruption of the intricate ecological balance in the relational domain of languaging, 'the house of being' in which our species becomes what it is – *Homo sapiens*. To live up to the *sapiens* ('wise') part of the name, we must, finally, let the elephant in the room out and follow the other elephant into the brave new world of which we are an inseparable and very important part that *does* make a difference. Let us try and make sure that this difference helps sustain the harmony in the world of the living rather than destroy it.

Let us become friends with elephants. *Let us understand language.*

References

Bateson, Gregory (1972). *Steps to an Ecology of Mind: Collected Essays in Anthropology, Psychiatry, Evolution, and Epistemology*. Northvale, New Jersey: Jason Aronson Inc.

Cooke, Michèle (2016). The elephant in the room: Communication, chaos and the translation of truth. In Richter, Julia; Zwischenberger, Cornelia; Kremmel, Stefanie & Spitzl, Karl-Heinz (eds.), *(Neu-)Kompositionen. Aspekte transkultureller Wissenschaft*. Berlin: Frank & Timme, 59–76.

Di Paolo, Ezequiel A.; Cuffari, Elena Clare & De Jaegher, Hanne (2018). *Linguistic Bodies: The Continuity between Life and Language*. Cambridge, MA: The MIT Press.

Everett, Daniel L. (2005). Biology and language: A consideration of alternatives. *Journal of Linguistics* 41, 157–175. https://doi.org/10.1017/S0022226704003093

Gibson, James J. (1979). *The Ecological Approach to Visual Perception*. Boston, MA: Houghton Mifflin.

Givón, Talmy (2009). *The Genesis of Syntactic Complexity: Diachrony, Ontogeny, Neuro-cognition, Evolution*. Amsterdam, PA: John Bejamins.

Kravchenko, Alexander V. (2011). The semantics vs. pragmatics debate in the context of the orientational function of language. In Kiklewicz, Aleksander (ed.), *Język poza granicami języka II. Semantyka a pragmatyka: Spór o pierwszeństwo*. Olsztyn: Uniwersytet Warminsko-Mazurski w Olsztyne, 11–23.

Kravchenko, Alexander V. & Payunena, Marina V. (2018). Практика в плену теории: почему так трудно научиться иностранному языку в школе. [Practice held hostage to theory: Why it is so hard to learn a foreign language at school.] *Tomsk State University Journal of Philology* 56, 65–91. https://doi.org/10.17223/19986645/56/5

Maturana, Humberto R. (1970). *Biology of Cognition. BCL Report # 9.0*. Urbana: University of Illinois.

Maturana, Humberto R. & Verden-Zöller, Gerda (2008). *The Origin of Humanness in the Biology of Love*. Exeter: Imprint Academic.

Morris, Charles W. (1938). Foundations of the theory of signs. In Neurath, Otto; Carnap, Rudolf & Morris, Charles W. (eds.), *International Encyclopedia of Unified Science*, Vol. 1, Part 2. Chicago: University of Chicago Press, 1–59.

Sharov, Alexei A. (1992). Biosemiotics: Functional-evolutionary approach to the analysis of the sense of information. In Sebeok, Thomas A. & Umiker-Sebeok, Jean (eds.), *The Semiotic Web 1991: Biosemiotics*. Berlin & New York: Mouton de Gruyter, 345–373.

Sinha, C. (2015). Language and other artifacts: Socio-cultural dynamics of niche construction. *Frontiers in Psychology* 6. https://doi.org/10.3389/fpsyg.2015.01601

Michael En

Of bullet points and cows: Illuminating truths and truisms

The link is not, in fact, missing. The link is the fact that we – translating humans, Homo transferens, are a part of the world, and not apart from it. It is only by recognising this fact, that we could not have evolved and continued to exist without this fundamental connection, that the ability to translate becomes comprehensible and logical.

The Missing Link

Tea recommendation for this chapter:
Everyday, with a big, mellow gulp of milk or your favourite dairy-substitute drink.

'I'm not sure you can become a translator. You'd need to learn all the words for describing how a blast furnace works!' – This was my French teacher's reply to my telling her, in the last year of my time at the *Gymnasium*, that I was thinking of studying translation after my *Matura*. I was one of her best students, and we liked each other, but apparently, her confidence in me to become what she imaged a translator would be was not strong enough for her to give me her blessing (or encouragement), and she figured a warning would be needed instead. Young me, who did not have any idea of what studying translation would require or entail, and who relied entirely on his teacher's feedback for assessing his own language (and many other) skills, was startled and felt insecure.

A few years later, I was indeed learning industrial furnace terminology in French. And I had indeed been told, including at university, that that was what I had to do to *become a translator*. But luckily, at that point, I already knew that that was not *what it's all about*. Because while some of my classes at the (University of Vienna's) Centre for Translation Studies were based on ideas of translation 'competence' very similar to those of my former French teacher, I had also attended classes by Michèle Cooke. And there, I had learnt a few crucial things that had nothing to do with furnaces, or rather, not with furnaces in particular. Instead, they had to with, well, *everything*.

And within that *everything*, Michèle led me to many realisations, illuminations, insights and revelations – relating to translation and also life in general. Often, these appeared as simple truths about life, which would, once I realised they allowed for an entirely new angle to describe the complexity of life, change mine. Here's my attempt at changing yours a little, too.

Learning from cows?

One of the first things I learned when I dipped into Communication Studies is that, as the saying goes, *we cannot not communicate* (Watzlawick, Beavin & Jackson 1967:51). It was through Michèle's teaching style that I truly learned that this means that everything we do is part of our communication. And that includes every aspect of how we teach. However, not everyone shared my enthusiasm for Michèle's way of communicating herself at university. Indeed, I kept hearing complaints about the presentation slides Michèle used in her lectures. These complaints were mostly framed with the following argument: 'Diese Folien kann man nicht lernen.'

If the absurdity I see in this isn't obvious to you right away, maybe my translating it into English will help, not only in case you don't understand German, but also in case you don't see what irks me about this. A possible translation would be 'You can't study with these slides.' – But the 'with' here is already helping the English version be more open to various interpretations. After all, 'study with' can be a lot of things; the preposition opens up a series of options that are missing in the German closer-knit, direct *Akkusativ* construction. The German version relies on the idea of 'lernen' both as 'study' and 'learn', even 'learn by heart' (or 'by rote', rather), and applies it to presentation slides. English options such as 'studying with' and 'learning from' do not restrain as much; 'studying the slides' would be something different altogether; so maybe 'You can't learn the slides' as a foreign-syntax translation might actually be best to get across my irritation with this expression here.

In this view, one is imagined reading – learning – presentation slides as one does with a book, say, a textbook made for preparing you for a specific exam. So those who felt frustrated in their attempt to 'die Folien lernen' saw the lecture as preparation for an exam (and not much more) and wanted to 'learn the slides'. They were happy with slides such as the one shown here as Fig. 1 (which they got in many other lectures, as I can attest to from my own experience).

They didn't know what to do with slides like the one shown here as Fig. 2.

Now, you might notice two things here. First, the difference in style between the two slides. Second, the cow.

Fig. 1: A slide, in the style many students apparently have come to expect (sadly, unfortunately, regrettably; seriously, doesn't it make you frustrated just looking at it?)

Fig. 2: A slide, Michèle style (imitation)[1]

---

1   The sentence featured here in this imitation is one that I would argue to be representative of Michèle's general lecture structure. Some English translations I can offer for it

I have to say, during my time as an undergraduate student, I saw a lot more cows and learned a lot more facts about cows than I had anticipated. Cows have been with me through all my transcultural life[2] – their role in etymology[3]; analyses of their positions and prototypical depictions in different cultures; the differences in onomatopoeia in different languages[4]; and, in Michèle's classes, their faces on presentation slides and discussions of what happens to you (emotionally) when you look into their eyes.

Let's take a good look at the two slides as communication. Which one do we 'learn from' *more*, or rather, *how* do we learn from them, and *what*? If students who see these slides learn that everything we do is part of how we communicate with others, and that therefore, as (future) experts for communication, we need to make conscious decisions about everything in our presentation of ourselves and our work, then how come there are those who do not understand why slides can and do look like this, and what to take from that? It seems that there are those who learn – want to learn – about communication, yet are confused, angered even, when they encounter it in unexpected forms such as forms of expression of what is taught (the very *putting into practice* whose lack translation students are said to be so often complaining about).

This idea of a lack of useful information that can be studied – easily absorbed – to be put to use in the neoliberal marketplace also features in recent critiques of *Wissenschaftlichkeit*. Not only do we now have a debate about what counts as 'science' as opposed to its others such as 'the humanities' or its marked cases such as 'social science' (something Michèle has continuously commented

---

here are 'What does that have to do with us?' and 'How does this relate to us?' or even 'How is that relevant to us?' …

2   As an example for unfortunate pronunciation choices reported, allegedly, from Truman College (Overheard Everywhere 2014) goes, 'Everyone has cows in their life. Cows at home. Cows at work. Cows in our families. Cows can take over everything. But how do we get rid of the cows?' – In this case, by pointing out that a lot of confusion can be avoided if one does not pronounce 'chaos' that way.

3   One example, which Michèle has used illustratively in various places, is the Irish word *bóthar* for road (hence also my use of the term in the *Einleitung*). It comes from the Proto-Celtic word for 'cow path' and is said to have been used to refer to a path broad enough for two cows to pass one another.Hence also my use of the term in the *Einleitung*.

4   For example, Wikipedia (n.d.) lists, among others, English 'moo', German 'muh', Arabic 'ngoah', Bengali 'hamba', Japanese 'mō mō', Tagalog 'ungaa', Persian 'māy', and Czech 'bůů'.

on) but also on the question of what this 'science' – or *Wissenschaft* – is good for. Employability? Profit maximisation? Teaching to save the discipline? How about being able to appreciate the world around us just a little bit more, for example while looking up and taking in the landscape during an afternoon spent reading under a tree on a sunny mountain meadow?

What do we expect to gain from learning by rote bullet points that we do not get from a cow (one that is impetus or background for an actual discussion of 'the material' during the lecture)? Perhaps more importantly, what is lost, forgotten, dropped – or not even picked up in the first place – if all we have is bullet points and no cows (or clouds or flowers or rainbows …) at all?

We cannot not communicate is something that many who have heard it once seem to put aside as a truism. To them, it might seem foolish to keep coming back to what seems to be a mere basic fact of life without much further consequence. Yet this ignorance of its consequences is the very reason I see this truth as still so important. If we take this statement seriously, we cannot simply go about our business as if it were 'obvious anyway'. Because a) it isn't obvious to many, and b) once it becomes obvious to us, we need to acknowledge and commit to it fully, lest nothing change and the world – our presentation slide design – remain the way it was before.

It has often been my impression that many of those unmoved by such fundamental truths seem to be the ones who would most benefit from considering their consequences in all the big and small things in life. At least it would have helped them make better sense of Michèle's cow slides.

Stating the obvious?

During my time with the Students' Union at the Centre for Translation Studies, we ran an online forum that served, among other purposes, as a place for students to share *Mitschriften* (notes) of lectures with fellow students. One of the courses that students were required to pass early on in their studies was one focused on a basic introduction to Transcultural Communication, taught by Michèle. In one semester in particular, as the exam date approached, more and more students posted in the respective thread in the forum, asking for notes, summaries, a *Mitschrift*. Some who had been attending the lecture or who had attended it in previous semesters posted replies, saying that something like a definite *Mitschrift* would be hard to produce, referring to the literature that the lecture built upon, to the material available online, etc. But confusion prevailed among many: Why was there no long, complete set of notes by anyone? What had the slides (of, among others, cows) to do with the reading list? Where were the bullet points?

Finally, someone posted a document with 'a summary of everything discussed in the lecture' to the thread. Those who downloaded and opened the file were presented with an almost empty page on which there was only a single sentence: 'People from different cultures and backgrounds see the world in different ways.' In the following posts, different emotions were expressed via words and emoji: some eye-rolling, some angry, some (especially those who had attended the lectures and understood instantly) delighted.

If someone asked me – as some of the students reading that *Mitschrift* did – if that was 'really all' the lecture was about, then I would eagerly say yes, and hasten to add that this 'all' is really a very big 'all'. To make this more explicit in the *Mitschrift*, maybe we could add to it: 'People from different cultures and backgrounds see the world in different ways – and that has a number of important consequences.'

The struggle becoming visible here is, again, between those who encounter statements such as the 'summary' in the *Mitschrift* in their approach to translation as a silly truism that doesn't offer the promise of new knowledge to be gained, and those who realise that as an insight, rediscovered and applied seriously, it allows you to deconstruct and reconfigure your entire perspective on and in life.

Both seminars on so-called 'intercultural training' and courses that are part of a university programme on transcultural communication take the idea that 'people from different cultures and backgrounds see the world in different ways' as a starting point or basic principle. However, while the former approach teaches you *the dos and don'ts* of, say, a business dinner with 'the French' or negotiating with 'the Japanese' so you can internalise them and be done with it, the latter allows for the complexity of being human, opens up critical perspectives and leaves you open, vulnerable, never fully complete. What makes the difference between truism and truth is not found in the idea itself, but in what we make of it.

The *Mitschrift* story also demonstrates the idea that that which is not or/and cannot be put into a 'studiable' (and perhaps 'examinable') format is not something we can learn from (including academically) or is somehow less informative, less serious, less important than those methods of teaching and thinking about the world that lend themselves better to, as discussed above, bullet pointisation. Michèle herself has said a lot on this in various talks and her work in general.

I see this as a question of science communication more broadly, relating to debates about what proper academic conduct should look like, and how one should approach students in a time where they are set up to be seen and treated as customers of the university as an institution deeply entangled in the pressures and violence of profitability in capitalism.

As Michèle puts it in her text on 'why science needs poetry':

> The purpose of poetry (or indeed any communication) is to impart a degree of otherness. It is only this way that we can experience other realities. [...] Scientists can be poets. We can adopt the artistic mode without sacrificing validity or truth, without telling non-truths or distorting the facts. [...] Scientists need to embody the facts before they can express them – need to think them, feel them, care about them. Only then can we put them out there for others to see and to care about. (Cooke 2012, 107–113)

And when we really *care* like that, can we fully share and communicate our caring in the form of bullet-point lists? Personally, as someone who is convinced that learning by rote specific definitions of concepts and the names of their assigned authors for exams is not useful, I was always immensely grateful when I had the pleasure to be welcomed into a topic – in lectures, presentations, videos or books; by Michèle as well as by others – with such *poetry* applied. You get ideas presented to you in enticing ways that refer to the full spectrum of human experience, not only using our ability to follow logic, our eyes and ears, but allowing us to grasp ideas fully with our bodies, which react – as anyone who's ever read a good book that they couldn't put down before the last page knows – with emotion, with joy, surprise, shock – and suddenly, you know a little bit more, you understand, you feel understood.

Getting it right?

Consider the following two texts about parents' reactions to their grown-up children leaving home. One is an excerpt from an academic article about 'empty nest syndrome', the other is a poem by British poet Pam Ayres about her son's going off to university:

> The process of "launching" children from the parental home (i.e., the transition to the empty nest) and the response parents have to their children's leaving (i.e., the empty nest syndrome [ENS]) have garnered the attention of researchers in recent years. However, although much has been written about this phenomenon, empirical findings are equivocal. On one hand, research demonstrates that parents—especially mothers—experience deleterious effects when their children leave home. In this sense, it is assumed that parents experience a loss that is significant and profound—one that

results in negative outcomes such as depression, alcoholism, identity crisis, and marital conflict (Bart, 1971; Curlee, 1969; Hiedemann, Suhomlinova, & O'Rand, 1998). On the other hand, empirical evidence suggests that the empty nest is a positive time for parents (Rubin, 1992), an opportunity for reconnection and a time to rekindle interests (Dennerstein, Dudley, & Guthrie, 2002; White & Edwards, 1990). Yet others go so far as to question the very relevancy of the ENS as a key concept in understanding the midlife experiences of parents (McQuaide, 1998). Indeed, midlife is a very extensive and diverse stage of the life course that can span up to at least 30 years (Lachman, 2004). (Mitchell & Lovegreen 2009; please see the paper for the references in this quote)

A September Song[5]

He is off to university, all is now in place,
There is fear, anticipation and excitement in his face,
An overstuffed enormous bag and rucksack in the hall,
And a ghastly leaden feeling like the ending of it all.

I cannot let it show, this selfish aching in my heart,
For the sweet chaotic years in which you played the major part,
I am fearful of the emptiness when you depart the room,
And silence settles round us like the stillness of a tomb.

At your bedroom door I used to stand and shake my head
The mess was unbelievable, the floor, the chair, the bed,
The place was never hoovered, never felt a duster's touch
But now it's neat and clean and I don't like it half as much.

I loved you going out, so young and eager and alive,
I loved you coming home, your little car turned in the drive,
The energy, the racket, all the songs you like to play,
And I won't know where to turn to when the music dies away.

There was ringing of the mobile, there was tapping of the text
The iPod and the iPad and the new thing coming next,
There was passion, there was fashion, with your father in despair
Saying, 'IN the name of GOD, what has that BOY done to his HAIR?'

Now parents realise that all between them that has dwindled,
Can be resuscitated and romantically rekindled,
Old passions reignited, sexual energies uncurbed,
But looking at your Dad, I think I'll leave them undisturbed.

---

5   'A September Song' from 'You Made Me Late Again!' by Pam Ayres, first published by Ebury Press © Pam Ayres 2013. Reproduced by permission of Sheil Land Associates Ltd.

My son is ready, independent, eager, fit, he *has* to go,
He must take his chances now! I know, I know, I know, I *know!*
He will make so many friends, he will be having such a ball,
It may all be so exciting … that he won't come home at all.

I am looking at a life which seems so drained of all its colour,
The heart is gone from us; we are older, we are duller,
Now if people ask us, we'll show photographs and say,
'He's up at university. That's right. He lives away.'

Which text is 'better'? Which one is more accurate? More 'true'? From which text can we learn more about the reality that both of them refer to? Do they even refer to the 'same' reality? How would we present what we have learned from them on a slide or in notes meant for others to 'learn with them'? Does one call for a list, the other for a picture of a cloud? Both? Neither?

Science – as every aspect of our experiencing and making sense of the world – needs poetry, not only in the form of verses and rhymes, but the *Poesie des Lebens*: the beauty that is not just the ray of sunlight as it travels through space reaches the Earth –

Computation procedure [for extraterrestrial illuminance:]

$$E_{XT} = G_{SC}\left\{1 + 0.034cos\left[\frac{2\pi}{365}\,(n-2)\right]\right\}$$

[…] As sunlight passes through the atmosphere, a portion of the incident radiation is scattered by dust, water vapor, and other suspended particles in the atmosphere. This scattered light from the sky is divided into three categories: clear, partly cloudy, and cloudy. Either the sky ratio method or the sky cover method is normally used to classify the sky. (Kandilli & Ulgen 2008).

– not just the warmth we feel when it touches our skin or the Vitamin D it enables our bodies to create –

[…] the formation of [³H]previtamin D3, [³H]lumisterol, and [³H]tachysterol after exposure of [³H]7-DHC to sunlight in Boston in June beginning at 1130 h EST. The amount of each ³H-labeled photoproduct in the irradiated solution is expressed as a percentage of the tritium recovered after HPLC. The assay was able to detect changes of as little as 1.0 ± 0.1 % ($\pm$SE) when run in triplicate. After only 2 min of exposure to noontime sunlight previtamin D_3 was detected. After 5 min 2 % of the original [³H]7-DHC was converted to [³H]previtamin D_3. […] [³H]Lumisterol and [³H]tachysterol were first detected after 30 min and 1 h, respectively. While [³H]lumisterol continued to accumulate during the next 2 h to 10.8 ± 0.3 %, [³H]tachysterol remained relatively constant at about 3 % after the first hour[.] (Webb, Kline & Holick 1988)

– and also not just the way we look up to the sky and say 'hey, what a nice day' to ourselves or the people around us –

> [...] speakers feel entitled to assume (at least within the UK context) that weather/environment conditions will draw similar, convergent responses from their listeners. Listeners will agree that a sunny day is 'nice', rain is 'horrid' or 'nasty', winter cold is 'bitter' and heat waves 'unbearable' [...] More dynamically and discursively, it is striking how speakers design their comments about the weather to elicit evaluative consensus. [... T]he principal weather-evaluating utterance is structured as 'it's ADJECTIVE isn't it?' [...] The tag question with falling tone seeks confirmation of an uncontroversial claim, and each of the cited instances draws confirmation from the next speaker in the following turn. (Coupland & Ylänne-McEwen 2014)

– but all of these and more taken together, shaken, mixed, experienced.

After all, what good does it do if we research and write about any matter that is close to our heart in a way that then forces us to try to take our heart out again, or to pretend it never was in it in the first place? As others have argued much more brilliantly – see, for example, Haraways' (1988) analysis of 'the god trick' or Shildrick's (1994) analyses of 'strategies of closure and exclusion which [...] are taken as categories of the real' – we are not serious if we're pretending to be able to be fully serious; and if we're genuinely concerned about the effects we fear to be brought about by not being (or appearing) impartial, neutral, 'objective', we should better do what we can to become aware that we're always and cannot help but be partial, biased, 'subjective' (cf. Bauer 2006; Collins 2000; Haraway 1988; Harding 1991).

If we see the result of our being human in all activities – including doing research, science and writing – as 'damage', then taking our subjectivity into account is the best way to mitigate this damage. Let's make the best of it – and given that it is part of our being and doing anyway, why not drop notions of 'damage' and 'loss' and instead celebrate it?

If we allow it to, translation can serve as a great example for this. Consider Translation Studies' move away from complaining about the burden of the fundamental impossibility of translation, the loss it brings and the faults it introduces, toward conceptualising translation in a way that allows for celebration – of the lightness of its mundane being possible, of what it makes possible, of its unique features. Just as we can stop seeing translation as an always-lacking inferior imitation that is caught between different forms of failure (as we know it from different models and metaphors) and approach it instead as ubiquitous (Blumczynski 2016) and a fact of life (Cooke 2011), we can embrace our humanity in the same way, ubiquitously informing our every doing – being our very being – that we cannot (and shouldn't want to) – escape – 'even' (or rather, especially) in our making sense of the world.

When our work expresses our specific passions (our *poetry)* already in its shape and form[6], we, as readers, gain something from that. We learn differently – even more? – about the topics discussed. Nick Sousanis (2015) published his doctoral thesis on the primacy of words over images in Western culture and ways of knowledge construction in the form of a comic titled 'Unflattening'. Patrick Robert Reid Stewart (2008) wrote about the influence of indigenous knowledge on architecture in a style chosen to honour Aboriginal people's oral traditions, writing without punctuation or uppercase letters, arranging paragraphs in various shapes, and mixing English with Nisga'a. In both these examples, we do not get a bullet-point list to learn by rote or even a neatly laid-out page with 'proper' formatting. Instead, we are offered an opportunity to understand in other, in additional ways.

And maybe that's exactly that what helps us get 'it' – and even more than that, allow us to see it, to experience it, to make it part of our own doing, necessarily so, as we are engaging with it in the moment. Bullet points are predictable and keep us safe; cows, on the other hand – well, nobody knows what cows are up to.[7]

So, should we drop all 'scientific' writing, all 'serious' academic style, all slides with bullet points? Yes. And no. There is definitely a need to break out of the straitjacket of academia, of being accused of being too personal in our approach, of letting our history influence our views, interests and knowledge. But as with

---

6   For reasons of brevity, please forgive me the implication that 'form' is what happens 'already', that is, 'before' content, or rather, that such a distinction between shape/form and content is one that should be made in the first place. The macro and the micro, appearance and substance, written words and the thoughts we think when we read them are false dichotomies, as are all dichotomies.

7   If you, for whatever reason, belong to the group of people who are afraid of cows (as indeed I have gotten to know more and more people with such fears), I apologise for this menacing phrasing. I know you don't trust the 'mountain sharks', as you might call them, but I hope you will allow them their place here in this text, helping me make my (non-bullet) point. Thank you.

any decision, we might find ourselves choosing to follow the travelled path, to play by the rules (or to pretend to for a while). Expanding one's range of options does not mean forgetting about those options that were there before.

Knowing the answer?

We can answer the question of 'which is better?' here with the one answer that, as every student of Michèle's knows, is often overlooked but always correct. The answer that is, as I like to see it, the *supercalifragilisticexpialidocious* of answers: *It depends*.

And oh, there is so much that things can depend on – and they always do. Once you realise that things really don't have to be the way that they are (or often seem to be), it seems ludicrous to answer any question ever with anything other than *it depends*. Because it's true – *it depends*, everything depends, it depends on everything. Who are you? *It depends*. What am I like? *It depends*. What does this mean? *It depends*.

Again, when we don't dismiss this idea as a useless truism right away, its powerful consequences for our every doing become clear. It is not only useful for teaching the basic counter-intuitivisms of translation – How do you say 'yes' in German? What is the right translation for 'nein' in English? *It depends*. – but has ground-breaking consequences for how we approach the world. It helps us deconstruct our enculturation, lift the veil of our own cultural gaze, and ready ourselves not only for all that is out there – different cultures, different ideas, different people and their different ways of life – but for what could be.

The rhetorical question about how much space we would have available without cars that one can find on stickers and in graffiti form all over Vienna[8] is an urban translation of answering the question 'How many cars *are there* / *have to be* in the city?' with *It depends*. And indeed now, in the wake of climate change/catastrophe, there are more and more efforts, sanctioned by the local government, to drastically change the numerical answer to this question.

It depends reminds us that things are not what they seem and, crucially, can help us remember that this has consequences – for us, for our lives, for what we do and what we don't do – that we tend to ignore or forget.

---

8   'Wie viel Platz wäre hier ohne Autos' – sometimes with a question mark, but I prefer it without one.

Fig. 3: Excerpt from Winston Rowntree's 'Anomalies', one of favourite comics from the Viruscomix 'Subnormality' series

If something that looks exactly like a closet door is not a closet door, what is it? What is the difference between a 'small, windowless room where things are stored on hangers for future use' and a 'closet'? Can we call a closet door that isn't one a closet door? Should we? What does the 'possibility' of encountering a non-closet-door closet-door mean for us and our encountering other doors, other non-doors, other others?

The full power of *it depends* shows itself when we use it to answer those questions in life that we are told only have one – single and/or correct – answer. How do you live your life? Who are you? Who do you fall in love with? etc. Saying *it depends* when faced with these questions takes courage, and often leads to confrontation, confusion, anger and all forms of violence.[9]

This is not to say that we should stop at *it depends* and never strive for any other, specific answer, but that we need to remind ourselves of this very specificity of *every* answer, no matter the context. (Really *every* answer? *It depends* …) That includes questions of a scientific-philosophical kind as well as social-moral questions (How many bones are there in the human body? What is a fact? What does the word 'Feuerwerk'[10] mean? How should we raise children? Is it a good idea to differentiate between 'scientific-philosophical' and 'social-moral' questions? …).

The difference between a superficial truism and a profound insight lies in what we do with it. If you're #teambulletpoint[11], you might not see what should be so exciting about something that is obvious anyway – *eh klar* – and, not seeing how this could matter, move on. But if you dare to take it seriously and apply it, critically, deeply, to the very aspects of your life that you might feel at first it is the most obvious in, it breaks your ground. And this ground-breaking – chipping away bit by bit, pebble by pebble, stone by stone the what you had been led to assume was solid, unshakable ground below you, digging and reaching for the other side or centre of the Earth, until you realise there is no other and no centre, and all you want to do is take the mud and build a sandcastle – can start with something as simple as a statement in an introductory class on Transcultural Communication. *Is this a translation? It depends.*

---

9   If you find this hard to believe, just talk to people who have said, in various forms, *it depends* in relation to their gender, their sexuality, their nationality, their home or any other facet of themselves and their reality that others deem fixed, unchangeable, defining. And by 'violence', here, I do not only refer to physical acts. Many forms of violence show themselves, as Panti Bliss puts it in her brilliant and moving TEDx talk, in 'all the little things' (TEDx Talks 2015).

10 I chose this example here not simply to put pretty explosions of colours in your reading mind but because 'fireworks', as straightforward as its 'meaning' seems to be, is already beginning a change in its use, e.g. in reference to visual effect shows produced only with the help of lasers and/or drones as alternatives to pyrotechnics-based (maybe-soon-to-be-called 'traditional') fireworks.

11 I feel obliged at this point to make clear that I am not opposed to bullet points as such. *Au contraire*, there are few things I appreciate more than a good list – for to-dos, for sorting out messes, for whatever the need.

In this spirit of *the need for poetry*, here's my take on the *it depends* of words and meaning:

Poem by a word

Some see me as a vessel
that's filled when read or spoken
which is redeemed for meaning as
a signifying token

Some see me as the ultimate
– of God, of law – authority
and yet if I'm to be divine
why don't I last eternally?

Some have debates about my form
where do I start, where do I end?
which version of me is the norm
and what's there that's equivalent?

If I'm at all a thing and fixed
then why do people say I've changed
I'm not what I once used to be
and sound, to many, foreign, strange

Some say, you can take mine for it
that's all that counts in changing times
others claim that I am cheap,
smokes and mirrors, hollow rhymes.

They've changed you, cry the critics
you don't make sense now anymore
but if you cannot handle me
then what's it that I'm really for?

Sometimes I am forbidden
sometimes not said aloud
and yet my absence – as my presence –
says what's it all about

If 'mean' is not a good thing
then why is that what I should do
if there's a chance that I am free
would you not want to try me, too?

Some say, that is too complicated
you're simply there, and that's the gist
but I am, take my word for it,
not even sure I do exist

                                                     – a word

Is that a useful take? *It depends.* Not because 'nothing matters' but because we leave room for potential. After all, we do not know, echoing Sean Thomas Dougherty[12], which *shapes of our words* will match the wounds of our readers/ listeners/watchers/… but letting *it depend* can lead us to new shapes, sometimes for wounds of which we hadn't even been aware.

Was hat das alles mit uns zu tun?

I'll leave this mosaic unfinished, as it has to be, and hope you enjoyed looking at the tiles I've laid down. Finishing this text, will you have 'learned' less than you would have done if you had read the academic essay I almost chose to present here instead?[13] I suppose *it depends.* In any case, I hope you got *something out of it*, or *something to put in.* Even if you stop worrying about slides and all and just look into a cow's eyes … who knows which truths you will see in there?

Was hat das alles mit uns zu tun? It depends. Moo.

References

Bauer, Robin (2006). Grundlagen der Wissenschaftstheorie und Wissenschaftsforschung. In Ebeling, Smilla & Schmitz, Sigrid (eds.), *Geschlechterforschung und Naturwissenschaften.* Wiesbaden: VS Verlag für Sozialwissenschaften, 247–280.

Blumczynski, Piotr (2016). *Ubiquitous Translation.* New York & Abington: Routledge.

Collins, Patricia Hill (2000). *Black Feminist Thought: Knowledge, Consciousness, and the Politics of Empowerment* (2nd ed.). New York & London: Routledge.

Cooke, Michèle (2011). *The Lightning Flash. Language, Longing and the Facts of Life.* Frankfurt am Main: Peter Lang.

Cooke, Michèle (2012). Ode to Joy. In Cooke, Michèle (ed.), *Tell It Like It Is? Science, Society and the Ivory Tower.* Frankfurt am Main: Peter Lang, 105–126.

---

12 See Dougherty's poem 'Why Bother?', published in 'The Second O of Sorrow', 2018, BOA Editions.

13 You will be able to compare someday, actually, as I intend to publish that essay elsewhere. At the moment, though, I can only refer you to En (forthcoming, someday, somewhere), which I realise is not very helpful.

Coupland, Nikolas & Ylänne-McEwen, Virpi (2014). Talk about the weather: Small talk, leisure talk and the travel industry. In Coupland, Justine (ed.), Small Talk. London & New York: Routledge.

Haraway, Donna (1988). Situated knowledges: The science question in feminism and the privilege of partial perspective. *Feminist Studies* 14(3), 575–599.

Harding, Sandra (1991): *Whose Science? Whose Knowledge? Thinking from Women's Lives*. Ithaca: Cornell University Press.

Kandilli, Canan & Ulgen, Koray (2008). Solar Illumination and Estimating Daylight Availability of Global Solar Irradiance. *Energy Sources Part A* 30(12), 1127–1140, https://doi.org/10.1080/15567030601100688

Overheard Everywhere (2014, 7 June) *Hamburgers, That's How*. https://overheardeverywhere.com/archives/104.html

Sousanis, Nick (2015). *Unflattening. A Doctoral Dissertation in Comics Form*. Columbia University. Harvard University Press.

Stewart, Patrick R. R. (2008). *Indigenous Architecture through Indigenous Knowledge*. PhD thesis. The University of British Columbia. https://open.library.ubc.ca/cIRcle/collections/ubctheses/24/items/1.0167274

TEDx Talks (2015, 8 January) *All the Little Things | Panti | TEDxDublin*. [Video]. YouTube. https://youtu.be/hIhsv18lrqY

Watzlawick, Paul; Beavin, Janet Helmich & Jackson, Don D. (1967). *Pragmatics of Human Communication. A Study of Interactional Patterns, Pathologies, and Paradoxes*. New York: W. W. Norton & Company.

Wikipedia(n.d.) *Cross-linguistic Onomatopoeias*. https://en.wikipedia.org/wiki/Cross-linguistic_onomatopoeias#Animals_with_cloven_hoofs

Webb, Ann R.; Kline, Loren & Holick, Michael F. (1988). Influence of season and latitude on the cutaneous synthesis of vitamin D_3. Exposure to winter sunlight in Boston and Edmonton will not promote vitamin D_3 Synthesis in human skin. *Journal of Clinical Endocrinology and Metabolism* 67(2), 373–378. https://doi.org/10.1210/jcem-67-2-373

Benjamin Schmid

The music in a name: Intersemiotic translation and musical cryptography

Poetry, like music and painting, thrives on space.
The space between the words or the notes, between objects,
between light and shade, is what gives any work of art its meaning.
This meaning is of necessity fluid.
We must each find our way to it and through it.

Ode to Joy

Tea recommendation for this chapter:
Mango Strawberry or your favourite fruit-mix infusion.

This text is not what it seems. It looks very much like an academic article because that's the format I'm used to when writing about translation. But actually, I like to think of this text more as extended liner notes to a song I wrote in homage to Michèle Cooke. That piece of music is the main text I'd like to present to you here, and this article is merely intended to explain how I went about composing it and what this has to do with translation – in this sense, what you're reading is a paratext that accompanies the song, if you will. The tune I've written is an intersemiotic translation, a translation between different media and different sign systems. It's built from notes and chords that I derived from the letters that make up Michèle's name. To do that, I used a form of encipherment called musical cryptography, which I'll explain in more detail below.

So I'd like to encourage you to read this text as liner notes to the music, if you're inclined. First, take a couple of minutes to look at the sheet music for the song at the end of this article and listen to my interpretation of the tune on my SoundCloud page at *soundcloud.com/benno_continuo/michele*. Then go ahead and read this article to find out how I composed the song, which different levels of intersemiotic translation are at play here, and what this little intersemiotic project can tell us about music as translation and music as a metaphor of translation.

In this text, I would like to cast a spotlight on how I went about transforming Michèle's name into music and to explain why this process felt very much like translating a text to me. I will start by providing some background information to put what I did into context: I'll briefly talk about how music is not only a metaphor of translation but also a medium for intersemiotic translation between different art forms and sign systems – like the translation that I'm writing about here. Then I'll look more closely at *how* I did it: I'll explain the concept of musical cryptography and talk about the creative choices and layers of interpretation that were involved in the process of composing, performing, and recording the song "Michèle".

Music

I know that music is important to Michèle, and this also shows in her writings. Her book "The Lightning Flash" (Cooke 2011) is structured like a musical work, with a prelude, a number of impromptus and variations, a finale, and two encores. In the book, Michèle touches on several aspects where music and translation converge: She writes about when the words of an opera or song matter and when they don't, how the emotional struggles of the speechless Rusalka in Dvořák's opera are expressed by the harp, and how the interplay between silence and sound is what makes music meaningful to us. She also looks at the ways in which the name popularly given to Chopin's Prelude Op. 28, No. 15 – the "Raindrop" prelude – can at the same time guide and restrict, enhance and narrow the listener's experience of the piece. Michèle is a lover of music, and she sees music as a way of translating our experience of the world for others.

Music is also very important to me, and it has played a central role in my life, particularly in the form of the bass guitar. In my life, there have always been songs that meant a lot to me and were like guiding lights or companions along the way. When making music and listening to music, I can go to places I couldn't access otherwise. Music has shaped my life, and it has also allowed me to experience a very unique form of non-verbal communication with the friends and fellow musicians I've played and jammed with over the years.

So it only felt fitting to me to contribute a piece of music to this festschrift, while, at the same time, taking a look at translational aspects of music composition, interpretation, and performance. Music and translation are connected in many different ways – here, I'd like to write about two of them: intersemiotic translation between written language and music, and music as a metaphor of translation.

Translation

As a teacher and a researcher, Michèle encouraged me, as well as many others, to extend my curiosity and my academic interests beyond the confines of "translation proper" – which was especially important for developing my own approach to and understanding of translation, both as a profession and as an object of study. Michèle already advocated a broad concept of translation at a time when the general consensus on what is and what is not translation was still much more rigid and restrictive than it is today, thanks to a growing body of research on intralingual and intersemiotic translations, so-called "cultural translation", and other non-canonical forms of translation.

One key aspect that was discussed many times in Michèle's research seminars was the question of where metaphorical concepts of translation stop and where "actual translation" begins. Much of Michèle's work and the work she inspired and supervised has interrogated and redefined the line between metaphorical and non-metaphorical uses of the concept of translation, and it has also questioned the reasons why such distinctions are made.

Many types of communicative transformation were previously regarded as metaphors of translation – as "translation" in quotation marks – but have now come to be recognized as actual, non-metaphorical translation. For example, many writers have compared science communication to translation. But Michèle was one of the first scholars in Translation Studies to genuinely conceptualize activities like communication across scientific and academic disciplines and the communication of science to non-specialist audiences as real translation in a non-metaphorical sense (cf. Cooke 2004, 2007). Similarly, all the many different forms of communicating specialist content to non-specialist audiences were long regarded as "somehow like translation", but have since become the subject of a growing body of work on intralingual translation in all its different (non-metaphorical) manifestations (cf. e.g. Schmid 2017:34–41, 2012; Korning Zethsen & Hill-Madsen 2016). And we're also seeing similar developments in the fields of multi-modal and intersemiotic translation and in areas of translation research that put an explicit focus on the translation of cultural perspectives, practices and identities rather than verbal/linguistic elements.

Slowly but surely, the concepts of translation discussed in Translation Studies have become richer, redefining the boundaries between what is thought to be "like translation" and what is recognized as actual translation. My little exercise in musical translation in homage to Michèle Cooke that I'm presenting here is my own way of playing around with these shifting boundaries, using a medium I enjoy.

Music as a metaphor of translation

First, let's look at the metaphorical side of things. Even though many aspects of musical performance and composition are very similar to processes involved in translation, in-depth discussions of music as an analogy of translation seem to be relatively few and far between in Translation Studies. Koller (1972:44–46) provides an overview of statements about translation that are based on the music metaphor. Musical performance and translation are both framed as art. While some of the statements listed by Koller place more emphasis on reproduction, others highlight processes of creative production involved in both music and translation (Koller 1972:46). Eduard (forthcoming) provides a number of more recent examples where musical terms and expressions are used as metaphors of translation. She argues that music provides a complete conceptual metaphor that covers many of the key characteristics of translation, placing special emphasis on the element of interpretation that is at the heart of translation and music. Gross (1991) highlights the usefulness of musical analogies for better understanding translation and interpreting. In particular, he likens the work of interpreters and translators to that of composers, performers, improvisers and musical archaeologists. As he says, "the beat is far more subtle than many can hear, and at any moment the translator may need to alter this beat, play another instrument altogether, launch into a prolonged improvisation, or even recompose a large part of a piece from scratch" (Gross 1991:34).

St. André (2010:5–6) provides a brief discussion of how music can serve as a "root metaphor" of translation that can branch out into sub-metaphors and cover many different aspects of translation. He notes that while a musician's performance is bound to the score (the source text) by certain musical rules, no two performances of a piece are alike, and there is considerable space for interpretation (as a case in point, St. André cites Glenn Gould's different interpretations of Bach's Goldberg variations) and also for improvisation in different musical traditions. St. André concludes that the root metaphor of music can be seen as empowering because it frames the translator as an artist.

Music as translation

Activities like composing, interpreting and performing music are not only seen as mere metaphors in Translation Studies, however. Recent research[1] on

---

1   This research is often located at the interface between Translation Studies and musicology, and it is represented by scholars such as the members of the Translating Music project (translatingmusic.com).

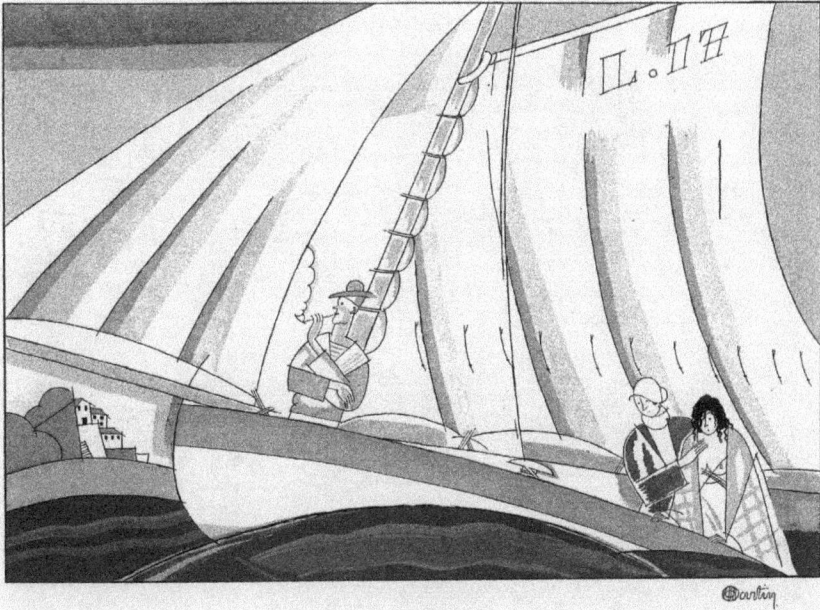

Fig. 1: Yachting by Charles Martin (Satie 1982; scan: Michael En)

music and intersemiotic translation looks at musical transformations and analyses them as translation in a non-metaphorical sense. These translations are in many ways similar to what I've attempted to accomplish with the composition I'm presenting here, so I'll take a short look at some examples of intersemiotic musical translations that have been discussed in the literature.

Ingham (2012) analyzes how poem texts are transformed and reinterpreted through vocalization when they are set to music in songs. Minors (2013) discusses how Erik Satie "musically translated", as he himself put it, 20 etchings by Charles Martin showing popular sports and leisure activities of his day, like golf, fishing, hunting, yachting, etc. In his scores, Satie used musical and visual elements to imitate or reinterpret the etchings. For instance, he used V-shaped notation and musical symbols to recreate the V-shaped scene of someone swinging a golf club so hard that it shatters into bits in the etching "Le Golf". The composition "Le Yachting" uses swelling arpeggios that symbolize the rising and falling ocean waves and the rocking of the boat that is shown in the corresponding picture (see Fig. 1 for Martin's illustration and Fig. 2 for Satie's score).

Fig. 2: "Le Yachting" by Erik Satie (Satie 1982; scan: Michael En)

Stones (2013) discusses another example of a composer who used techniques of intersemiotic translation: John Cage. Cage placed great importance not only on music as sound but also on the visual qualities of the scores. He is regarded as one of the pioneers of graphic notation, i.e. the use of symbols other than traditional musical notation to write down music, driven by the need for new types of notation capable of accommodating the new techniques and improvisational elements found in 20th century avant-garde music. These developments added a whole new visual dimension to musical scores. In his 1969 book "Notations", Cage highlighted this emerging field of visually oriented musical notation, including examples from his own scores. Cage was both a composer and a visual artist, and his work inhabits an in-between space where music and the visual arts converge. Fig. 3, a section of the score for the experimental piece "Water Walk" illustrates this in-between quality.

Moss (2013) looks at a piece by the Estonian composer Arvo Pärt, who translated his experience of Anish Kapoor's sculpture "Marsyas" into music. In his

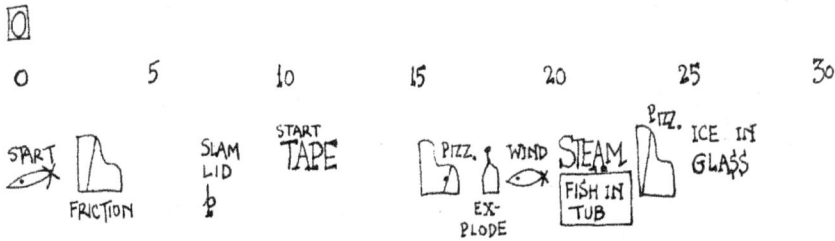

Fig. 3: A section from John Cage's "Water Walk", an example of graphic notation (scan: Wikimedia Commons)

piece "LamenTate", Pärt sought to reexpress through music the sorrow, pain, and passion he felt when contemplating the sculpture (Moss 2013).

Another example is presented by Yeung (2008), who discusses the loop of intersemiotic and interlingual translations that surround Gustav Mahler's composition "Das Lied von der Erde". This piece uses lyrics adapted from Chinese Tang poetry, which were translated back into Chinese in 2002 to be incorporated into a modern Chinese choreography intended to translate Mahler's music into dance.

These are clear examples of how artistic techniques and aesthetic effects have been translated into music from other media. This is also what I have done in my tune "Michèle". But even if no clear elements of intersemiotic transformation are involved, any process of musical composition and performance requires processes of interpretation and creation on many different levels – as Desblache points out, "music is intrinsically dependent on translation in its broadest sense" (Desblache 2018:323) because composing, performing, and listening to music all imply multiple, complex interpretations (Desblache 2018:314).

Here, my goal is to illustrate some of these complex interpretations that were involved in translating a name into music.

Musical cryptography

My first step in composing the song was transforming the letters of Michèle's name into musical notes. To do that, I used a mechanism called musical cryptography.

Throughout the history of music, various methods have been developed for enciphering words and messages by turning them into musical notes and symbols. The most common way of doing that is to assign letters to different notes

Fig. 4: The Bach motif

based on a code that is known only to the sender and the receiver of a message. This makes it possible to encrypt texts in the form of music. There are several historical examples of musical cryptography being used to hide secret messages in pieces of music – these examples range from the papal cryptographic service to the French diplomatic service and musically encrypted criminal correspondence that was intercepted by the New York Police Department. Some of these encryption systems reached remarkable levels of complexity (for an overview and details, see Sams 2001:753–754, Shenton 2008:69–80 or the entertaining video on musical cryptography available on the music theory channel "12tone" on YouTube (12tone 2017)).

But – and this is more important for understanding the song I'm presenting here – there is also a long history of musical cryptography being used as a compositional device, as an artistic technique for creating music. When musical cryptography is used for artistic purposes, the goal is usually not to transmit a secret message, but rather to create pieces of music that contain a reference to some non-musical content, an intertextual relation to a name or a literary text, etc. Composers use musical cryptography to create multi-modal art that establishes a connection between music and written language.

The most obvious approach for turning words into music is to encipher messages using the letter names of the notes in the C major scale (in English: C, D, E, F, G, A, B). When we start the scale from A, the notes of the C major scale give us the first seven letters of the alphabet.

The most famous example of musical cryptography where a name is spelled out based on note names is the Bach motif. This motif takes advantage of a specific feature of German musical notation, where the note B is called H, and B flat is called B. This gives us an additional letter to work with (H), which makes it possible to spell out the name Bach in the form of musical notes.

This musical cryptogram was used by Johann Sebastian Bach himself and by many composers after him who wanted to add a reference or nod to Bach in their works. This short motif shows how encipherment establishes an intertextual link – it links the musical text (a four-note motif) to another text in a different medium (the name "Bach"). This type of intersemiotic translation creates a special relationship between the notes and non-musical symbols: It gives new meaning to what would otherwise be only a simple sequence of notes. In this way, musical cryptography imbues the motif with a reference to the name "Bach", activating all the potential dimensions of meaning a listener or reader of the music might associate with this name. Someone who is aware of this link is likely to interpret music containing this motif differently, because the musical cryptogram adds an additional layer of potential meaning to the notes.

The approach of using the note names of the C major scale to spell out names is very basic, and it's limited to only a few letters – but still, it has been used quite frequently, most notably by Bach, Brahms, and Schumann. But, unsatisfied with the limitations of this approach, other composers went on to develop more and more complex systems of musical cryptography (see Sams 2001:755–757, Shenton 2008:69–81).

There are numerous examples of composers who developed their own systems of musical cryptography, from Michael Haydn and Arthur Honegger all the way to progressive metal guitarist Ron Jarzombek, who devised a cryptography system of his own for enciphering his name in the song "In the Name of Ron" (from the album "Solitarily Speaking of Theoretical Confinement"; Jarzombek even developed a smartphone app called "Play The Name" that allows users to encipher their names into music based on this system).

The famous French twentieth-century composer Olivier Messiaen developed a particularly elaborate system of musical cryptography. His system uses fixed pitches and note lengths to represent all the letters of the alphabet (see Shenton 2008 for an in-depth study of this system). In addition to these letter ciphers, he also included a number of musical formulas to represent grammatical cases and auxiliary verbs. Messiaen called his system of musical cryptography *langage communicable* ("communicable language"). In his organ work "Méditations sur le Mystère de la Sainte Trinité", Messiaen combined this *langage* with additional semantic elements (including liturgical chants, transcriptions of birdsong, and symbolic leitmotifs) to translate entire passages and theological ideas from Thomas Aquinas' "Summa Theologiae" into music (for details, see Shenton 2008).

The "Michèle Cooke" cryptogram

When I sat down to compose "Michèle", I started by looking for a satisfying way of enciphering the letters of Michèle's name. The German note names (C D E F G A H) gave me three letters of the name (C, H, E/È), but I had to look elsewhere to find note representations for "MI" and "L", the parts of the name not covered by the German nomenclature. I didn't have to look too far, though: I simply used the Romance system of musical notation that uses syllables as note names: Do, Re, Mi, Fa, Sol, La, Si (in technical music terminology, these are known as solmization syllables). These solmization syllables provided the missing letters: "Mi" (the Romance name of the note E) and "l" (I stretched things a bit and simply dropped the a from La, the syllable corresponding to the note A in English). The full "Michèle" note sequence now looks like this:

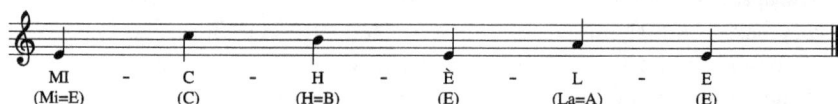

| MI | - | C | - | H | - | È | - | L | - | E |
| (Mi=E) | | (C) | | (H=B) | | (E) | | (La=A) | | (E) |

Fig. 5: The "Michèle" sequence

Things get a bit trickier when we're trying to encipher the last name, "Cooke". The note names of the C major scale only give us a C and an E. But what to do with the two Os and the K? German notation doesn't help us here, and neither do the Romance solmization syllables. Fortunately, there are alternatives: I turned to what's known as the *clef anglaise* (see Shenton 2008:74), another system of musical cryptography frequently used by well-known composers, most famously Maurice Ravel (see Shenton 2008:74; Sams 2001:756).

A	B	C	D	E	F	G
H	I	J	K	L	M	N
O	P	Q	R	S	T	U
V	W	X	Y	Z		

Fig. 6: The clef anglaise

Just like the basic system that uses English note names, the *clef anglaise* includes the seven first letters of the alphabet as they appear in the C major scale, starting from A. But then it starts over again and maps the next seven letters of the alphabet on the same sequence of notes. This procedure is repeated until all letters of the alphabet are covered (see Fig. 6).

The advantage of this system is that it's not too complex, but still allows us to encipher all the letters of the alphabet, not only the first seven. The disadvantage is that the cipher is ambiguous, because in the *clef anglaise*, a single note can represent up to four different letters. I chose this system nonetheless, because it is easy to use and to explain, and also because it was popular with a number of famous composers.

The *clef anglaise* allows us to represent the O with the note A and the K with the note D. We can add these ciphers to the C and the E we get from the basic note names, and, voilà, we now have a complete "Cooke" cryptogram to work with.

	C	-	O	-	O	-	K	-	E
	(C)		(A)		(A)		(D)		(E)

Fig. 7: The "Cooke" sequence

So far, the process of composing has involved a fair amount of what could be described as transcoding – I've applied formalized rules to transfer elements from one semiotic system to another. But some interpretation has been involved, too: I had to choose the cryptographic methods I thought would work best, and I mixed different methods to obtain the results I needed for composing a piece of music that I hoped would not sound too alien to most listeners' ears. So even at the encoding stage, the process involved interpretation and creative choices intended to achieve certain effects.

The cryptograms provide the raw material for the composition, but the result is just a list of notes, not a piece of music. I needed to make many more artistic choices to build a chord progression and a melody from these raw building blocks.

The chords

The song "Michèle" is actually a twofold musical cryptogram: My goal was to derive not only the melody notes from the letters of Michèle's name but also the chord progression. I wanted both the melody and the root notes of the chords to spell out the name. When I sat down to turn the note sequences into a song, I started to work on the chords before I developed the melody.

In very basic terms, a chord is what happens when two or more notes are played at the same time. The distances between these notes (i.e. the intervals) give the sound of the chord a certain quality (e.g. major vs. minor, etc.). Chords define the harmony of a song and can perform certain functions – they can sound restful, destabilize the harmony, introduce tension, resolve tension, etc.

The role chords play in music is in many ways similar to the role concepts play in communication: The chord names on a sheet of music are outlines of musical ideas, they enshrine potential musical meaning that can be actualized in different ways in different musical contexts. How a chord sounds and which function it has in a song depends largely on the chords that come before and the chords that follow.

In jazz sheet music, chords are usually represented by chord names – an E minor chord can be written as Em and a C major seventh chord as Cmaj⁷ (once again, there are many different systems for writing chord symbols). These symbols are abstract – they represent a certain sound quality, a basic idea of what the structure and the function of the chord should be, but there are many different ways of playing any single chord, and it's up to the performing musician to interpret the chord. A chord symbol (loosely) defines a group or pool of notes that, when they're played together, create the sound of a particular chord. Especially in jazz and other improvisational forms of music (for example the *basso continuo* style of harmonic accompaniment in baroque music), it is to a large extent up to the performer to decide which notes of a chord to play, and in which order (this is called the voicing of the chord). In jazz, the performer can also add further notes to a chord to add more color to the sound (extensions) or replace it with an alternative chord that expresses a similar musical idea (chord substitutions). These types of creative decisions are required for turning a chord name written on a sheet of music into actual sounds. This is just one example of the many translational processes involved in the performance of music.

When I wrote the chords to "Michèle", I wanted the root notes of the chords to follow the "Michèle" and "Cooke" sequences. So it was clear that I had to start the song with some kind of E chord. The type of E chord I would place at the beginning and the end of the parts would define much of the basic tonality (the key) of the song. I chose E minor, because the note C from the "Michèle" and "Cooke" sequences only appears in the E minor scale, and not in E major. Plus, the "Michèle" cryptogram begins with the solmization syllable Mi – this is another argument for choosing minor over major, because minor is often abbreviated as "Mi".

So I started with an E minor chord and developed the chord progression from there. I mostly used a spontaneous or, if you will, intuitive approach: I simply played around with different possibilities (different types of C, B, E, … chords, different chord durations) until I came across something that sounded right. Whenever I was happy with a passage, I would build from there and develop the harmonic progression of the song further.

There were also some theory-guided elements at play in the writing process, however: For instance, I tried to achieve what musicians call efficient voice leading – this means that I tried to make the different voices contained within the chords flow smoothly from one chord to the other, without abrupt jumps. I also tried to find a compelling (or at least pleasant) movement in the bass voice, and I aimed for chord movements that would slowly build up harmonic tension and then resolve the tension back to a sound that feels at rest (this is a key feature of European music and musical traditions influenced by European music).

Finding good chords for ending the "Michèle" and "Cooke" parts proved to be particularly challenging. I wanted to find something that would allow the performer to loop the parts, i.e. to start over from the beginning after reaching the end of a part. This was a problem because the sequences end with E chords, which are then followed by another E chord (E minor) at the beginning of the "Michèle" part when the song starts over. Sitting on a chord at the end of a part and starting over using the same chord is problematic because the root note stays the same, which means that there is very little harmonic motion going on when the new part starts, resulting in a transition that can feel too weak in a song such as this one. I solved this problem by using so-called slash chords at the end of the parts. Slash chords are chords that are played over a bass note that is different from the root of the chord. This allowed me to end the parts on E chords, but special variants of E chords that include a fair amount of tension and that sound different enough from the "vanilla" E minor at the beginning of the song to achieve a (to my ears) satisfying harmonic resolution.

In the "Cooke" chord progression, I also used another technique for building up harmonic movement towards the end: With every chord change, I sped up the harmonic rhythm (the duration for which a given chord is played). The C chord at the beginning is played for two full bars, then the two A chords for one bar each, and the D and E slash chords that conclude the part are only played for half a bar each.

The melody

In some ways, finding a melody for the song was easier than coming up with the chords. I didn't have to start from a blank page, and I already had the basic structure of the tune. I could let the chord progression guide my choices in writing the melody. I took the notes of the "Michèle" and "Cooke" sequences and tried to place them on top of the chords in a musically meaningful way. I mostly followed an intuitive "play around with the notes until it sounds right" approach. I recorded the chord progressions and played them in a continuous loop, while trying out different melody lines on the bass until I found short phrases that I liked. I then used these bits as starting points to develop the melody further.

But again, the process also involved some theory-guided decisions: I spaced out the melody in such a way that the most important, sustained melody notes hit chord tones (i.e. notes that are part of the chord over which they are played).

The many E notes and E chords added some extra challenges. When you play the melody note E over an E chord, you hit the root note of the chord, which in many contexts can sound a bit boring. For this reason, I tried to avoid placing a long, sustained melody E over an E chord wherever possible. This is the reason why some of the melody phrases in the song draw out the penultimate note. The final E is then played only very briefly as a pick-up note leading over to the beginning of the next phrase (for example in bars 2 and 4).

The end result of all this enciphering is the musical cryptogram you see in Fig. 8 – a song in E minor with an A part where the root notes of the chords spell out "Michèle" and a B part where the chords spell out "Cooke". The A part melody consists of the "Michèle" note sequence repeated three times over, followed by the "Cooke" sequence. In the B part, the melody is built from the "Michèle" sequence followed by the "Cooke" sequence, each played only once.

I hope these glimpses of my writing process show that this intersemiotic translation was not a simple transcoding exercise – at each step of the process, I had to make creative choices under the formal constraints of musical cryptography and the stylistic norms of "Western" music (socio-cultural norms and traditions).

The jazz lead sheet

I present the song "Michèle" to you in the form of a jazz lead sheet (Fig. 8 at the end of this text). The lead sheet is a particularly translational format of musical notation. Performing written music always involves a degree of interpretation – you can't simply play "what's written on the page", because what's written on the page is symbols, not music. To turn the symbols on the page into music, the performer has to interpret them, and, based on this interpretation, deliver a performance. Actual musical performance always involves many more aspects than can possibly be notated on a sheet of paper. The music on the sheet does not determine the actual music as it is performed and enjoyed by different players and listeners, much like a written text does not determine how it is interpreted by different readers, and how it is translated by different translators.

In the world of classical music, performers can become famous for their own special interpretations of the pieces they play – for their expressive use of tempo, rhythm, dynamics, timbres, etc. Even in electronic music, the artist has to decide how the notes should sound, which wave forms, textures, timbres, sound effects, rhythmic patterns to use, etc. Any type of musical performance requires creative choices to be made, depending on the performer's aesthetic and stylistic approach, and in this sense, performing written music always means translating it from one medium into another.

In many types of classical music, the sheet music usually specifies the exact notes to be played. Very broadly speaking (there are exceptions), classical musicians interpret the music primarily by choosing *how* they play the material. Jazz lead sheets, in contrast, give great freedom to the performers and require them to make constant choices about *what* to play. A jazz lead sheet presents the basic outline of a song – the chords and the melody. The chords provide a basis for accompanying the melody, but they can be played in many different ways. Similarly, the melody notated on the sheet is also treated more like an outline or a point of reference – the performers are free to modify and elaborate on what's written on the lead sheet. Some research results suggest that the different focus on how vs. what to play may even be reflected in different brain activity patterns found in classical and jazz musicians (Bianco et al. 2018).

The prominent role of the performer-as-interpreter in classical music, jazz, and many other musical traditions and styles is an interesting aspect when we consider that the relationship between source text authors and translators is often compared to that between composers and performers – which throws into relief the difference in status between these two complex interpreting-based activities.

Writing down tunes in the form of a jazz lead sheet allows for a remarkably broad range of interpretations, which can sound radically different from each other. For example, in their recording of Dizzy Gillespie's famous bebop tune "Salt Peanuts", saxophonist Steve Coleman and his band Five Elements radically change the meter and stylistic character of the song, but it's still accepted as a version of "Salt Peanuts". There are countless other examples: On the album "Anthem", Ralph Towner recorded a stripped-down, reharmonized acoustic guitar version of Charles Mingus' mournful ballad "Goodbye Pork Pie Hat", orig-inally performed by a jazz quintet. Joni Mitchell, in contrast, put lyrics to the song and performed it with a large electric jazz band on her album "Shadows and Light". Radical interpretations and reinterpretations of jazz standards are the norm, and performers are expected to add their own personal twist to the standards they play (cf. Lawn 2013:37).

Jazz itself is no longer a clear-cut genre today. It has become a very open idiom, with stylistic conventions that have become fluid and flexible. It can accommo-date many different approaches and aesthetics – a whole world of possibilities, with improvisation as one of its (few) universal characteristics. This is another reason why I decided to write down "Michèle" in the traditional format of jazz notation – to allow maximum freedom for interpretation.

But the layers of interpretation and translation in music don't stop here. They go beyond composing and performing, involving many other aspects that are far too diverse to discuss here. Let me just briefly mention two other translational dimensions of music that are relevant to the song I'm presenting to you.

Soloing as translation

Playing a solo over a chord progression is a very personal musical statement, an expression of the soloist's experiences, musical identity, taste, intuitions, spon-taneous ideas, preferred patterns of playing and ways of thinking. All of these factors can influence the choices soloists have to make when navigating through the structure of a piece of music and weaving their own melodic ideas into the music. I believe it's not too far-fetched to say that soloists translate themselves into the music in a very real sense. I wanted to add this translational aspect to my own recording of "Michèle", so I included a solo, which, I hope, contains some of my own musical identity.

Recording as translation

Recording a musical performance means translating the music to tape (or, more likely, hard disk, or whatever medium is being used). This statement is often in-tended as a metaphor, but there is also a significant amount of non-metaphorical substance to it. Recording music requires creative choices on many different levels: deciding on the instrumentation, choosing between different recording techniques (live, overdubs, etc.), and selecting the appropriate equipment (instruments, microphones, amplifiers, etc.). And then there are the countless sound-processing tools and effects that are available in the studio. One can shape the timbres and frequencies, add space to the recording by using reverb and echo effects, manipulate the stereo image of recording, and much, much more. The creative possibilities are almost endless. For example, it's possible to translate a piece of music into the aesthetics of 1980s pop music by using the signature sounds and studio techniques of that era (e.g. generous amounts of strong but short reverb added to the drums).

Your way to it and through it

After discussing all these layers of translation involved in composing and recording "Michèle", I'd now like to propose a challenge to you: If you enjoy the ideas and the song I've presented here, and if you feel like it, take the lead sheet (Fig. 8) and translate the piece into your own musical language. Make it your own. And if you do, please be sure to get in touch and share the results with me.[2] I'd be thrilled to see you continue this chain of musical translations with your own interpretation. As Michèle wrote, "The space between the words or the notes, between objects, between light and shade, is what gives any work of art its meaning. This meaning is of necessity fluid. We must each find our way to it and through it" (Cooke 2012:109).

Special thanks

I'd like to thank André Müller (andremu.com) for his help in fine-tuning two of the trickier chords in the song, Celia Martín de León for pointing me to relevant literature, and Michaela Chiaki Ripplinger and Michael En for their valuable feedback that helped me to improve this text.

---

2   Please write to benno.continuo@posteo.eu.

Michèle

Benjamin Schmid

Fig. 8: The "Michèle" lead sheet

You can listen to "Michèle" at:
soundcloud.com/benno_continuo/michele

Alternatively, you can also use the following
link: https://rebrand.ly/michele-song

You can also scan this QR code to access
the song directly.

References

12tone. (2017, January 17). *Musical Espionage and the Bach Motif.* [Video]. YouTube. https://youtu.be/CiS8gbkDISY

Bianco, Roberta; Novembre, Giacomo; Keller, Peter E.; Villringer, Arno & Sammler, Daniela (2018). Musical Genre-Dependent Behavioural and EEG Signatures of Action Planning. A Comparison between Classical and Jazz Pianists. *NeuroImage* 169, 383–394. https://doi.org/10.1016/j.neuroimage.2017.12.058

Cage, John (1969). *Notations.* New York: Something Else Press.

Cooke, Michèle [as Kaiser-Cooke, Michèle] (2004). *The Missing Link. Evolution, Reality and the Translation Paradigm.* Frankfurt am Main: Peter Lang.

Cooke, Michèle [as Kaiser-Cooke, Michèle] (2007). *Wissenschaft Translation Kommunikation.* Wien: Facultas.

Cooke, Michèle (2011). *The Lightning Flash. Language, Longing and the Facts of Life.* Frankfurt am Main: Peter Lang.

Cooke, Michèle (2012). Ode to Joy. In Cooke, Michèle (ed.), *Tell It Like It Is? Science, Society and the Ivory Tower.* Frankfurt am Main: Peter Lang, 105–126.

Desblache, Lucile (2018). Translation of Music. In Sinwai, Chan (ed.), *An Encyclopedia of Practical Translation and Interpreting.* Hong Kong: Chinese University Press, 309–336.

Eduard, Elizabeta (forthcoming). *Metáforas de la traducción: Análisis cognitivo de un corpus textual en lengua búlgara.* Doctoral thesis at the Universidad de Las Palmas de Gran Canaria.

Gross, Alex (1991). Some Images and Analogies for the Process of Translation. In Larson, Mildred L. (ed.), *Translation: Theory and Practice. Tension and Interdependence.* Binghampton: State University of New York at Binghampton, 27–37.

Ingham, Mike (2012). The Mind's Ear: Imagination, Emotion and Ideas in the Intersemiotic Transposition of Housman's Poetry to Song. In Raw, Laurence (ed.), *Translation, Adaptation and Transformation.* London: Bloomsbury, 188–209.

Koller, Werner (1972). *Grundprobleme der Übersetzungstheorie.* Bern & München: Francke.

Korning Zethsen, Karen & Hill-Madsen, Aage (2016). Intralingual Translation and Its Place within Translation Studies. A Theoretical Discussion. *Meta* 61(3), 692–708. https://doi.org/10.7202/1039225ar

Lawn, James L. (2013). *Experiencing Jazz*. 2nd ed. New York: Routledge

Minors, Helen Julia (2013). Music Translating Visual Arts: Erik Satie's Sports et Divertissements. In Minors, Helen Julia (ed.), *Music, Text and Translation*. London & New York: Bloomsbury, 107–120. https://doi.org/10.5040/9781472541994.ch-009

Moss, Debbie (2013). Music Mediating Sculpture: Arvo Pärt's LamenTate. In Minors, Helen Julia (ed.), *Music, Text and Translation*. London & New York: Bloomsbury, 135–148.

Sams, Eric (2001). Cryptography, Musical. In Sadie, Stanley (ed.), *The New Grove Dictionary of Music and Musicians*. 2nd ed. London: Macmillan, 753–758.

Satie, Erik (1982). *Twenty Short Pieces for Piano. (Sports et divertissements)*. Illustrations by Charles Martin. Mineola, NY: Dover Publications.

Schmid, Benjamin (2012). A Bucket or a Searchlight Approach to Defining Translation? Fringe Phenomena and Their Implication for the Object of Study. In Herrero, Isis & Klaiman, Todd (eds.), *Versatility in Translation Studies: Selected Papers of the CETRA Research Seminar in Translation Studies 2011*. https://www.arts.kuleuven.be/cetra/papers/files/schmid.pdf

Schmid, Benjamin (2017). *Leicht-Lesen-Übersetzungen und sozial perspektivierte Verständlichkeit: Eine Interview- und Paratextstudie*. Doctoral thesis at the University of Vienna. https://doi.org/10.25365/thesis.48526

Shenton, Andrew (2008). *Olivier Messiaen's System of Signs. Notes Towards Understanding His Music*. Ashgate: Hampshire.

St. André, James (2010). Translation and Metaphor. Setting the Terms. In St. André, James (ed.), *Thinking through Translation with Metaphors*. Manchester: St. Jerome, 1–16.

Stones, Alan (2013). Translation and John Cage: Music, Text, Art and Schoenberg. In Minors, Helen Julia (ed.), *Music, Text and Translation*. London & New York: Bloomsbury, 121–134.

Yeung, Jessica (2008). The Song of the Earth. An Analysis of Two Interlingual and Intersemiotic Translations. *The Translator* 14(2), 273–294. https://doi.org/10.1080/13556509.2008.10799259

Michaela Chiaki Ripplinger[1]

Is this the end of the era of human translation? Thoughts of a human translator at this curious time

> *Does MT [Machine Translation] have a future?*
> *This depends to a crucial extent on the willingness of MT researchers*
> *to venture beyond their computer-oriented environment*
> *and take a good hard look at what translation really is […].*
> *MT needs to admit the relevance of the difference between*
> *humans and machines. There is little point in investing*
> *enormous amounts of time and money*
> *if all you get is texts nobody wants to read.*

> Machine Translation and the human factor:
> Knowledge and decision-making in the translation process.

Tea recommendation for this chapter:
Lapsang Souchong, with milk or your favourite dairy-substitute drink.

Do translators have the blues?

When, in the fall of 2018, the then General Secretary of the Social Democratic Party of Germany remarked on a public TV show that many professions, among them translators and interpreters in particular, would soon be eradicated by artificial intelligence[2], it did not take long for translators' and interpreters'

---

1 I would like to thank Michael En and Benjamin Schmid for extremely helpful comments on various versions of this paper and making me aware of relevant literature and websites. I also thank Laura Scheifinger for proof-reading a final version of this essay. Arguments that have remained vague or any errors you might spot in the text are mine.

2 'Ich nehme mal nur das Beispiel der Übersetzer, der Dolmetscher. Kann ich gern länger ausführen, aber die wird es in ein paar Jahren als Dienstleister nicht mehr geben, weil technologische Entwicklung das überflüssig macht.' See BDÜ (2018).

professional associations to react arguing otherwise. Echoing argumentation also brought forward in other contexts, one of the profession's representative bodies in Germany pointed to how translation and interpretation demand was growing globally according to statistics[3]; argued that new technology had for centuries augmented translators' capabilities without replacing them, so technology was not to be seen as competing with human service providers; highlighted ethical reasons and the frequent sensitivity of content in some contexts, requiring translation and interpretation that excluded the use of technology; and lastly, said that machines had no common sense, which, in turn, enabled humans to spot logical mistakes that would fly under the radar of any computer program.

As a member of this profession myself, I felt gratitude for this solid response, but at the same time I could not help thinking that, of course, *they had to say that* – after all, lobbying for our case was their job.[4] The unease caused by what many perceive as a sharp rise in machine-translation capability is palpable in the industry as media reports keep hailing the rise of a technology that will free the world of the burden that is the human translator. There is the researcher-slash-developer group, whose lead author can be reached at a Microsoft e-mail address, that claims that the translation quality of their neural machine translation (NMT) system 'has reached full parity compared with the output of human translators' (Hassan et al. 2018). The *Wall Street Journal* enthusiastically announced that '[t]he language barrier is about to fall' (Ross 2016), reverberated by the slogan 'Goodbye Language Barriers' found on the website of a company selling 'earpiece translators' that provide 'accurate translations' in '20 languages and 42 dialects'[5], leading *The Economist* to conclude that 'translators have the blues' (Johnson 2017).[6]

---

3   The BDÜ ('Bundesverband der Dolmetscher und Übersetzer') press release cites a study by the US market research firm Common Sense Advisory (CSA) that predicts a continuous growth in the language services industry that will exceed 56 billion US dollar by 2021 (BDÜ 2018). Vieira (2018) points to a forecast by the US Bureau of Labor Statistics that predicts a growth in the translation and interpretation market by 18 % between 2016 and 2026.

4   Another example where the mentioned professional association felt it was necessary to point out that humans are still needed in the translation and interpretation industries stems from July 2019: https://bdue.de/aktuell/news-detail/bundessprachenamt-setzt-auf-menschliche-expertise-beim-uebersetzen-und-dolmetschen/ (accessed August 31, 2019, in German).

5   The quotes were taken from said company's website and its marketing materials: https://www.waverlylabs.com (accessed August 4, 2019). I thank Michael En for pointing me to this website.

6   I first encountered the examples of Hassan et al. 2018, Johnson 2017 and Ross 2016 in Vieira 2018.

As a freelance translator myself, I feel troubled in this 'brave new world' of labour that seems to be convinced it can do without what I view as my expertise. I consider myself part of a profession made up of people who believe that the words we choose can make a big difference and that attention to detail in language use is not a luxury when translating but the standard work mode of a professional. So, in a way, the doubt whether the work one is doing is good enough, the nagging feeling that there is always a little something to improve, is not really a novelty. What is new, however, is the sense of alarm translators feel that is caused by the increasingly widespread understanding that this expertise we are applying as professionals can easily be programmed into machines. As developers and market observers speak of 'parity' (a claim that is, incidentally, not corroborated by research on this topic, see, e.g., Vieira 2018 and Aragonés Lumeras & Way 2017[7]), translators can maybe not help but wonder whether machines are really getting better than they are. But better at what exactly?

Translation Studies scholars have been probing this uneasiness for a while now. They find that the advance in machine translation technology has been putting pressure on translators by lowering prices and enforcing agency's expectations regarding discounts for repetitions, etc. For business-minded people, there is no question that all available technological means providing the opportunity to technologise work should be readily employed by human translators.[8] Machine translation (MT) is now also used in more text types than in the past

---

7   Aragonés Lumeras and Way (2017) present a long list of shortcomings of MT in comparison to human translators but also emphasise that translators could gain much from incorporating MT in their work.

8   This is perhaps part of a larger trend that makes life harder for individual freelance translators while favouring agencies making money off the backs of lowly paid translators. The European Union's latest TRAD19 tender for translation (https://ec.europa.eu/info/tender/trad19_en, accessed August 31, 2019) reflects the dissatisfaction of one-person companies and individuals working in the industry: A public Q&A section (see link above) contains a number of comments criticising the fact that the EU has pledged to consider individuals or small teams of translators when outsourcing translation work, but by the way the call is organised and through the requirements for bidders, it is clear that only large agencies have a chance. This trend is also witnessed by Moorkens, who writes that the so-called vendor system in which large organisations such as the European Commission Directorate-General of Translation, 'one of the world's largest translation services providers', seeks to reduce its staff translators and increase the percentage of outsourced work from 25 % to 40 % (Moorkens 2017:466).

and in market sectors where MT-based translations were previously considered inappropriate (Moorkens 2017). This has an impact on pay, but pay is not the only way translators are affected: Vieira (2018) finds that translators are not mainly anxious about MT because of the resulting financial pressure but because of the effect on business practices MT brings about (which I will say more about in the next part).

The metaphor of a 'brave new world' I used myself in a previous paragraph seems unavoidable. It is also picked up by O'Thomas (2017) in his discussion of today's 'posthuman' world of translation. If translation could truly be realised in an adequate way by machines, he writes, this would have a huge democratising and liberalising effect on the world, as there would no longer be limitations on what is translated and who has access to translations. Yet, he also points out that translation practice and theory need to redefine themselves, as we are moving into an era where MT will be merged with human translation in such a way that it will, at some point, become impossible to clearly distinguish them anymore. In a world where the amalgamation of machines and human beings has already been realised in many fields, Translation Studies and translation practice need to reinvent themselves in order to survive and stay relevant.

Demystifying (or concretising?) the blues

But what exactly it is that machines can apparently already do when it comes to translation? In the previous part, I wrote that the professional association was saying what it had to say. But a closer look at the response reveals that it is not only eloquently phrased, it also shows that the authors of the press release took their research very seriously: They state that MT has improved significantly due to large databases, rule-based systems and particularly NMT, but that these improvements merely cover the translation needs humans alone cannot handle anymore and that the existing systems are far from being able to function without human input. And this argumentation is fully in line with what various very recent research papers report as the status quo of MT.

A special issue on the topic of human factors in MT[9] published in the summer of 2019 concludes that, for the time being, technology is far from being able to replace human beings despite the great advances in automated translation

---

9   Special Issue: Human Factors in Neural Machine Translation. Machine Translation volume 33, issue 1–2 (https://link.springer.com/journal/10590/33/1/page/1, accessed August 31, 2019).

(Castilho et al. 2019). What is more, the confident press reports that keep popping up in regular intervals do more harm than good by fuelling exaggerated assumptions and 'overselling the technology', which risks triggering negativity regarding MT, as systems cannot live up to the unrealistic expectations created this way (Castilho et al. 2017:118). And, more specifically, the current hype surrounding NMT[10] has to be viewed with some perspective (Kenny 2018).

To gain this perspective, it is helpful to take a look at the history of the development of automated translation. In the late 1990s, rule-based machine translation (RBMT) entered the language industries, which had until then snubbed MT due to its significantly lower quality compared to human translation. It is interesting to note that MT's commercial success took off at that time because a market had developed that had previously not been there. In the internet era (the era we are currently in), qualities such as immediate availability, mobility and ubiquity have acquired a significance they did not have before. As a result, a demand for translations where a certain level of linguistic 'inappropriateness' is considered acceptable in return for being 'mobile', etc. has developed. The resulting market for such translations has been termed the 'low-end market'[11] (see Kenny 2018).

---

10 NMT is, very simply put, corpus-based MT that makes use of a neural artificial intelligence network whose structure some authors compare to the structure of the human brain and that is designed to 'learn', i.e. become better based on the input it receives for every translation it produces based on matching target text and source text phrases. In comparison to NMT, statistical machine translation (SMT) is corpus-based MT that uses statistics to calculate the probability of a given phrase of a large corpus of texts matching a given source-language phrase. A somewhat more technical explanation of NMT is offered by Forcada (2017).

11 It should not be overlooked that such a 'low-end market' also gives rise to a market for professional translators. The automatic computer translations of patents freely offered by, for instance, Google helps potential clients identify documents which could be relevant to them, in which case they can order a reliable, human-made translation. However, such a low-end market and its pressures naturally are a source of anxiety for translators and particularly newer generations of translators. Kenny (2018) suggests three potential ways to react to this pressure that have also been pondered by translator trainers: Firstly, translators can decide to emigrate upwards and aim to serve high-end customers (an approach that is championed by, for instance, Moorkens 2017, 2018, who proposes to also incorporate this view in translator training). Secondly, translators can migrate their services downward (as suggested by Pym 2016, who believes that newer generations of 'translators', if the term is to be kept, should be trained accordingly). And thirdly, translators could seek to not become the experts that correct machine output once it has been produced but to strive for a location at the centre of the translation process, not serving but actively using NMT capabilities for their own purposes.

After its introduction in the late 1990s, RBMT was replaced by statistical machine translation (SMT) only a few years later. SMT was considered the state of the art from the mid-2000s to about 2015. Around the year 2015, NMT pushed SMT off the throne and has since been hailed as the hitherto missing link that would finally do away with the need for human translators (it must, however, be noted that SMT is still in use today). While NMT has in fact been able to produce further improvements in MT output quality, which had plateaued for quite a while with SMT and RBMT, Kenny (2018) for instance argues that NMT is a sustaining rather than a disruptive technology. In other words, while the output improvements achieved by SMT have really changed the translation industry in a disruptive way, NMT has had limited impact on the language industry's capabilities, methods and ways of doing things. With NMT, similar challenges have to be addressed as with SMT: A large amount of training data has to be provided and processed for NMT to work effectively; the systems must be designed in such a way that human intervention becomes possible for optimum results; and these humans, a new generation of translators, need to be trained in using NMT effectively.

So, in the current state of affairs, humans are not replaced by machines but we are not left alone by them either. Post-editing (PE), which Kenny (2018) reports has been one of the largest growing segments in the language industries even before the rise of NMT, has become a ubiquitous part of the translation world, with many translators already working in the field and PE being increasingly addressed in translator training. Pym (2013) believes all translators will become post-editors sooner or later. However, there is considerable resistance among human translators to accept the offers of MT and act as post-editors rather than translators.

Resistance against the uptake of new technologies is probably a very human trait. Moorkens (2017) mentions the widespread initial unwillingness among translators to introduce computer-assisted translation (CAT) tools, which today are widely accepted and almost universally used by professional translators. A difference between CAT and MT tools, however, is that CAT tools were designed to support translators, whereas MT is sometimes used to cut translation costs and push translators into handling assignments and delivering results in a way they find questionable (Moorkens 2017).

The resistance against the task of post-editing among translators is perhaps due to the great fluctuations with regard to the quality of the machine-translated text they are asked to repair or finalise. What is more, beliefs about whether automatic input can be of help or not influences how effectively translators use these tools. In a study comparing the task of editing an NMT-based translation with working with a classic translation memory, Gijón et al. (2019) observed that whether the use of technology made translators faster or slowed them down was linked to their expectations whether that would be the case or not. If a translator expected the MT input to accelerate their work, it did, and also the other way around. More generally, they found that the productivity boost expected as a certain result of the use of NMT could, at least at the moment, not be observed.

It must not be overlooked that the uptake of MT among translators is not entirely negative and strongly depends on how the people involved are treated. In their study on the use of MT among translators, Cadwell et al. (2017) report how surprised they were to see that acceptance of MT was not as negative as stated in many papers on this topic. Instead, among the translators they investigated, some even regarded MT as a source of inspiration. Cadwell et al. (2017) also found that human factors played a significant role in resistance against MT. In the two cohorts of translators they investigated, one was made up of translators working for a large translation agency who generally felt frustrated about having to deal with MT in their work. The other cohort consisted of translators working in an EU institution who were generally very satisfied with their work conditions. They felt that their work was appreciated and that they had a say in how the MT system offered at their workplace should be used. They also had the opportunity to provide feedback on the MT output, which was then used to improve the MT system. As a result, this cohort's response to MT was more positive compared to their peers', even though unease was part of both cohorts' responses:

> [The] emotional or affective dimension of MT post-editing needs to be considered. Both cohorts felt concerned about the negative influence that using MT can have on a translator's abilities in terms of blocking the translator's thought processes or creativity, of making the translator lazy, or of preventing the translator from being able to discern quality translation. Both cohorts also expressed a more general fear of the unknown with regard to how technology would develop and how MT might affect their working lives in the future.
>
> (Cadwell et al. 2017:312)

In post-editing, human input is required after the fact. But looking at the whole process of MT, human input is necessary even before and in order to produce automatically generated output in the first place. NMT, SMT and rule-based MT all require a corpus on which they are trained and from which they draw their material in order to produce their output. The way such corpuses come about and the question of how translators' input into such a corpus (that aims to make them redundant in the long run) is to be remunerated are some of the issues that will have to be addressed (see Moorkens & Lewis 2019). For translators working with such a corpus, the varying quality of the translations in the corpus is reported as a big issue. This is also linked to a further matter addressed by translators using MT: not knowing where a translation comes from (see Sánchez-Gijón et al. 2019).

In this context, it is also relevant to mention that the dimensions of the corpus required to effectively produce a MT are much larger than the ones professional translators or even small translation agencies possess. As a result, the use of NMT systems is practically reserved for large corporations such as Google or Booking.com, which already apply them in-house (Forcada 2017). Offers aimed at and affordable for freelance translators are, however, also on the market, for instance DeepL Pro[12], for which astonishing results are reported particularly in the German-English language pair.

So where does that leave us?

Machine translation and the human factor

I chose the topic of MT and the threat it is said to pose to human translators for my contribution to this *Festschrift* because this issue had been bothering me for quite a while (which is, see below, how you choose a topic of investigation according to Michèle Cooke). Just a little way into my thought process, I remembered that, as luck would have it, Michèle had also dealt with this topic – in her 1993 doctoral thesis at the University of Vienna, titled 'Machine Translation and the human factor: Knowledge and decision-making in the translation process'. To locate her work in the history of the development of MT, it can be said that it was produced a little while before rule-based machine translation produced first MT results that were considered somewhat acceptable. Yet, even though MT's success story had not yet started, Michèle identified in her thesis issues that have remained salient in the debate up to this day and which are addressed in various recent studies conducted to investigate the impact of MT on the work experience of translators and the interplay between human and machine in the field of translation.

It will not be a surprise to anyone who knows Michèle that her thesis about MT is essentially about the question of what translation *is*, or, as she puts it, 'what translators do and how they do it or, in other words, what they know and how they know it' (Cooke 1993:15). In the pursuit of this question, she argues that MT and Translation Studies ought to learn from each other instead of eyeing

---

12 See https://www.deepl.com/home (accessed on August 31, 2019). The German company also runs Linguee, which they refer to as the world's largest translation database.

each other with distrust. It is against this backdrop that she formulates the core
of her research question:

> Significantly enough, the three basic problems of MT also represent fundamental issues
> for translation theory:
>
> 1. Is meaning or anything else 'transferred' during translation? If yes, what and how?
> 2. What level of ST[13] understanding is necessary to enable adequate translation?
> 3. What does the translation process actually involve, i.e. what is the crucial difference
>   between monolingual analysis and generation, and analysis in one language with
>   generation in another?
>
> (Cooke 1993:11)

In answering these interrelated questions, Michèle debunks the notions that
being bilingual is equivalent to being able to translate, that a text can be translated without being understood ('the finished text can be regarded as verbalised
comprehension', ibid:90), that translating can be accomplished by matching individual expressions, that there can be such a thing as a 'literal translation', or that
a translation could ever be a 'translation in itself' instead of a translation with a
specific function. She explains that any text is only the surface expression of the
ideas an author aims to express and in order to translate a given text, a translator
must actively reconceptualise the ideas presented in it. In order to be able to do
so, translators must be able to recognise a given experience of the world expressed
in a different system of conceptualisation and to reproduce this experience in the
conceptual norms of the culture into which they are translating. Among other
things, this requires that they understand the text in a way that fits their understanding of a situation because conceptualisation is not only language-specific
but situation-specific. 'All this', Michèle concedes, 'may be terribly inconvenient
when working in the computer paradigm, but it is the explanation of what translating is and why translation can take place' (Cooke 1993:113).

In a chapter on target text, Michèle addresses the theory that in translation,
concepts remain constant and only the concept labels have to be exchanged:

> The first, spontaneous reaction to this is to ask – if it is so simple, why does it not work
> better, in machines and people? The second is that empirical evidence and introspec-
> tion seem to suggest otherwise. Incomprehensible translations are not just those where
> 'the grammar is all wrong', but those which look like English (for example) and feel
> like English, but still do not make any sense – why? Because they apply English rules

---

13   For readers from outside the Translation Studies field: ST stands for 'source text', i.e. the
     text that is translated, while the result of this translation is called the 'target text', or TT.

of syntax and morphology to 'invariant' concepts and recreate the coherence patterns
prescribed by these concepts.

(Cooke 1993:116–117)

This bears a striking resemblance to a comment made in Moorkens (2018)
regarding the type of mistakes common in MT. One of the participants in
Moorkens' study who were asked to post-edit SMT and NMT output commented
that there were fewer mistakes in the NMT output, yet they were harder to spot –
a fact that does not necessarily reduce the harmful potential of such mistakes,
contrasting the common-sense view that MT output quality is high when the
number of mistakes is low and the existing mistakes are not perceived as grave
(or even remain unnoticed) by readers. In light of the hailed improvements
regarding output quality generated in NMT and the oft-made observation, also
among translation experts, that MT really seems to be 'getting better', one cannot
help but wonder if this is in fact a surge in quality or whether errors are simply
being camouflaged more efficiently. Or have we all become so used to the idea of
a 'translation' being produced based on corpus equivalences without the involve-
ment of a human agent who has checked the text against their world knowledge,
understood it in its context and recontextualised it for a new target setting that
we accept such a translation into, say, English as long as it 'looks English'?

In her doctoral thesis, Michèle deals with the human factor of translation in,
among other places, a chapter dedicated to expert knowledge. Any attempt at
quantifying human knowledge and reducing it to factual knowledge in order to
cater to existing limitations of computers, she writes, robs it of the very traits that
make it human and valuable, namely subjectivity, uncertainty and the impreci-
sion of tacit knowledge. This is problematic because it is these very features that
help humans rationalise and objectivise experiences, also enabling us to avoid or
minimise uncertainty and error in comparable situations. What is more, the creative element of translation is not about recreating somebody else's text. Instead,
it is about 'producing a *different* text, [...] projecting the same situation from a
different perspective' (Cooke 1993:145, original emphasis).

This echoes the concerns expressed by the translators tasked with post-editing
MT texts surveyed by Cadwell et al. (2017), some of whom, as cited in the previous part, felt that the use of MT endangered their creative potential. Michèle
also specifically addresses this point when she writes about intuition, which, she
explains, is the term usually used to denote the tacit knowledge professional
translators rely on in their work. Intuition is 'where true expert knowledge
comes into play. Rule-following [...] reduces 'translating' to label-substitution
for fixed sets of concepts, to predictable, repetitive problem settings, and does

not allow for the *uniqueness* of every translation situation' (Cooke 1993:148, emphasis in the original was shown via underlining). Maybe times have changed so much that the ongoing commoditisation of translation services has really done away with a certain level of uniqueness in some translation assignments. In my opinion, doubt remains, however, whether that could ever be the case for the majority of translations required and produced and whether the narrow work setting in which post-editing is realised leaves enough space for the human beings tasked with this assignment to put their expert knowledge to use.

Technology has changed so drastically since the early 1990s that it is impossible to directly apply Michèle's assessment of the capabilities and limitations of MT to the systems available today. What is striking, however, is the fact that with regard to the *definition* of translation, at least for those of us who refuse to accept a neoliberal, commoditised understanding of translation along the lines of what certain participants in the language industries can efficiently (have) produce(d) and sell, the pressing questions have not changed all the much. And in her dissertation, Michèle already raised a lot of these questions.

What is a 'translation' according to society at large?

What we have seen so far is that MT has and will continue to impact human translators: what is expected of them, to what degree they are considered experts, the work conditions considered acceptable or sufficient, and, not least, what kind of view of translators society at large holds. These are big issues that are related to an even bigger question: What is viewed as a translation?

As with many definitions, what counts as a translation is notoriously flexible and Toury (1985) has famously said that a translation is whatever society accepts as translation in a given moment in time. In my doctoral thesis (supervised by Michèle), I have argued that communicative events can be actively designed to be perceived as translation in order to convey to the target group the feeling that they are getting 'direct access' to a given source text (Ripplinger 2014). In this process, an agenda of the communicating party is realised. Essentially, translation as a communicative act that takes place between different societal actors always involves power aspects, even when it pretends not to do so or when translators believe they are only producing 'another version' of what has been said by somebody else (in this case, the normative discourse has clearly won the power battle).

It is against this understanding of translation that I believe that the rise of MT will have a large impact on what society considers translation and, crucially, on the power issues involved in the emergence of potential new understandings of translation. *Somebody's* agenda will be served, and this will most likely happen in an opaque way (a 'natural' appearance of a text camouflaging its active, agenda-driven construction), present itself as innocent (particularly by pretending that an 'idiomatic, unmarked' translation is the 'correct' translation and thus the 'correct' interpretation of contents concerned) and require the scrutiny of experts with expertise regarding translation that is not superficial but exceeds the simplistic view of translation as 'saying the same thing in another language'.

Beyond the question of agenda, the view of translation in MT is based on the belief that 'similarity' of texts regarding their linguistic forms and organisation will result in a 'similarity' of communicative effects. This belief rests on the assumption of an unproblematic 'transfer' of a combination of words and concepts as well as the message this combination is understood to convey into another language. Translators know that this is often not the case: Saying 'the same thing' in a different context will convey the 'same' message only in very basic texts, along the lines of 'push button A in order to start operation B'. And especially in texts that are about the human experience, for instance marketing texts describing the appeal of a product, service or, e.g., tourist destination, it is questionable whether the feelings that are intended to be evoked by the text can be transported in a translation without a human being to note the possible feelings conveyed in the ST in the first place.

The fact that this very conveyance of a feeling is often achieved with passable effect by MT both astonishes and alarms me. Yes, we will probably learn that effective communication is more programmable than we previously thought. At the same time, I believe that this will in the long-term not be maintained or improved without tinkering with the notion of 'acceptable'. If we move into a future where translating means checking the acceptability of matches of text segments in two languages, the very fact that translation will be understood as the monitoring of degrees of 'equivalence', a highly contested notion in Translation Studies filling scores of pages of publications in the discipline, will surely have an impact on what we will view as a passable match.

This potential future scenario of what is considered translation is wildly at odds with my constructivist view of it, shaped by the notion that translation is meaning-creation, which has been long established in the discipline. If a view of translation prevails that sees it as a more mechanistic process, the time allotted to any given translation task will surely be affected by this, as will remuneration. The same goes for the reputation of the field's professionals, which is not about vanity but about the fact that reputation and being able to claim working conditions required to produce professional and high-quality results are closely linked.[14] What is more, such a view of translation conceals the fact that there is always an agenda involved in translation. It seems that some decades after we established in the discipline that 'translation is never innocent', we are returning to a view that assumes that at least some forms of translation are indeed 'neutral'.

Another issue that has to be considered with regard to society's view of translation is linked to the low-end market mentioned above. In this market segment, a translation that is barely understandable can be considered sufficient because all that is required for the translation to count as successful is a very basic grasp by its target audience of the ideas mentioned in the source text. This means that the low-end market is a low-expectations market. It remains to be seen how this low-expectations market will impact the market where a translation is only considered a high-quality translation if it effectively and smoothly communicates the message originally conveyed in the source text to a new target readership – the high-expectations market, if you will. Will both markets exist side by side in the future or will one type of expectations at one point become the standard view?

When future prospects for professional translators are discussed, it is often suggested that they should specialise on 'transcreation'[15] in order to not go out of business (see, for instance, Vieira 2018). This very suggestion – that translators should move into a branch of text production that is 'creative' – shows that a re-definition of what translation is, a re-definition that moves towards considering translation a process that is *not* creative, is already taking place. Again, returning to the concept of meaning-creation mentioned above, one cannot help but reassert that translation is always creative because it is creation. Yet again, moving forward, will translation one day be mere re-creation of 'matching' sentence pairs produced some time in the past and recycled for a new context, i.e. a purely non-creative process? It is hard not to be alarmed at this prospect.

Whose discourse?

Another concern related to MT is the question whose discourse is chosen for automatically produced translations. When statistics decide about the adequacy of a translational solution, a likely scenario is that whatever is conceived as correct

---

14 This becomes particularly clear when looking at conference interpreters' approach to professionalism as expressed in code of conducts. See, e.g. Setton and Dawrant 2016:357.

15 Transcreation most often refers to the adaptation of (primarily) advertising material for foreign markets. See Pedersen 2014 for a discussion of the concept and various definitions of transcreation and how they (do not) differ from translation.

by the majority will be given prevalence in texting decisions. The advances we are seeing in MT output in the past years are largely identified as a sharp increase in the correct use of grammar and idiomatic expressions. This is, of course, impressive, but there is a potentially dark side to it as well. When something sounds 'very idiomatic' or 'very natural', it sounds so because it is what many speakers of the language concerned would say without thinking about it. In other words, something sounds 'natural' because it is part of the majority discourse. This is particularly problematic when 'natural' is then automatically equated with the only way for a text to sound 'good'.

If this trend continues, translation will lose an important function it previously fulfilled. Naturally, not all translation assignments are suitable to provide the space to question the majority discourse and thus the majority view of given societal realities, but the slow and incremental input of a language-conscious breed of translators who are aware of the fact that language use impacts and shapes the world in which this language is used is not to be underestimated. This does not mean that translation has so far mostly been a battleground on which activist translators hammer home their messages while completely ignoring or sacrificing other communicative aims related to a given text to be translated. A language-sensitive approach to translation means that a translator is aware of the fact that no wording choices, and particularly not the ones labelled 'mainstream' and 'most widely acceptable', come without an agenda that serve the interests of specific groups and ignore or work against the interests of others – in the case of most 'mainstream' choices, the interests served are those of the groups in power. It is only based on this awareness that conscious language decisions can be made (which includes opting for the majority discourse) – a responsibility and creative power that is lost in any form of MT, as consciousness is not, at least as of yet, a capability machines possess.

In the past, less globalised world, translation was used to introduce new ideas to people in other cultures, sometimes even just by pretending to be a translation as witnessed by the phenomenon of pseudo-translations[16]. Translation was a way through which people in different cultures learned about each other and their achievements. And by looking at translation, it was possible to see how different cultures viewed each other. This opened up opportunities to analyse

---

16 Pseudo-translations are a phenomenon whose existence in various forms has been witnessed throughout history. Generally speaking, they are 'texts which have been presented as translations with no corresponding source texts in other languages ever having existed' (Toury 1995:40).

and critically reflect on the cultural interpretations that were available to people in a given culture of others. If the question of which discourse is chosen is one day no longer a question in translation because it is not considered relevant in an equivalence-based automated understanding of translation, the result will be the illusion that some translation choices are 'neutral', nobody's discourse and thus serve nobody's interests. This is a falsehood that is already widely believed by many – including, unfortunately, a considerable amount of people who translate –, and whose illusionary power will only be strengthened if MT develops as described.

Accountability

The third point I would like to touch upon is related to both the questions of agency and discourse as discussed above. If a translation is not produced by a person, the author of a translation (the translator), then who is responsible for the translation? Who can vouch for the fact that the contents that were identified as the relevant message of a given source text have been interpreted in a way that the intended target audience would agree with?

It feels reckless to flood the world with such texts that have no author without considering potential implications. A text is an act of communication because it enables us to understand what another person wanted to say to us. A text solely translated by a machine has no author. It is a text that was fabricated based on identifying chunks found in existing translations and deciding for an order in which to present the identified equivalent chunks based on similarities with other texts (see Aragonés Lumeras & Way 2017 for a highly accessible explanation of the procedures involved). Who is there to check what it is that such a text communicates to its readers?

Michèle once described translation as the willingness to see what somebody else sees. The willingness to stand in somebody else's shoes, to strive to understand the world as somebody else did. Of course, a machine or program does not stand in somebody's shoes or strives to relive somebody's experience. We keep seeing that, apparently, this is not necessary for some translations to work sufficiently. But what are the consequences of more and more texts being produced based on algorithms? What happens when nobody is responsible for a text because nobody wrote it?

Translations produced for a commercial purpose are frequently not only the product of the text's translator(s) but are altered by various editors along themanufacturing process of the final product. So also in traditional processes in the translation industry today, it is often oversimplified to localise authorship and the responsibility it entails with only one human being. And where MT output is already put to use, a post-editing human being is in most cases still involved. But as the translation industry seems to be moving into a more automated future, the questions raised in the paragraph above (for which I feel unable to propose even tentative answers) might at some point in the future become more salient than we ever considered possible.

Serving society

For a different research project I recently completed, I looked into the topic of professional ethics and codes of conduct for interpreters and translators. In this process, I came across an intriguing definition of what constitutes a 'profession' that departs from interpretations of ethics upheld by the AIIC and the professional associations and study programmes that follow the AIIC's lead when it comes to defining the 'ideal form' of the professional practice of interpreters. This definition of an expert profession proposed by Sedat Mulayim and Miranda Lai (2017) strays from most other definitions that are largely similar to each other. Mulayim and Lai write that opposed to a trade or craft, professional experts are defined by what they offer to society. They have a skill that others need and do not have themselves. This fulfilling of other people's specific needs is what makes and keeps them relevant for society. And this is also how they can gain reputation in society, which in turn enables them to safeguard the working conditions they need in order to provide good work. If you believe that something you are lacking is important to you, and you trust someone – an expert – to be able to deliver this something, you will be more willing to listen to what this expert says and believe them when they point out certain restrictions or needs. This understanding of being providers of a needed service, Mulayim and Lai write, should inform professional ethics codes that experts turn to when they come upon tricky questions in their professional practice.

It is in this vein that I believe that we, as translators and Translation Studies scholars, have to keep offering what we can. This includes our knowledge about how to produce good translations, translations that effectively communicate one human being's thoughts and beliefs to other human beings located perhaps far off, physically, mentally, emotionally, ideologically, etc. We should also help judge what counts as a good translation and what does not. And we should contribute our expertise and shape general understandings regarding what translation is to begin with. Much is going to change in the professional work of translators, some things for the better, others maybe for the worse. Translation Studies scholars, many of whom have tackled the question of what translation is all about ever since the discipline was established only some decades ago, are well-equipped and suitable and thus need to provide input that ensures that the human factor in translation remains seen despite the commoditisation that is likely to proceed.

In the end, nothing has changed about the decades-old insight in Translation Studies that translation is, always, a decision-making process. MT decisions are not made in a pragmatic way; they are 'not intended to be either linguistically or cognitively plausible (just *probabilistically* plausible)' (Aragonés Lumeras & Way 2017:23, original emphasis), but that does not change the fact that also a MT comes about based on numerous (mathematical) decisions leading to its production. Moving into a future where it seems plausible that many translations will only be based on machine-computed decisions, let's make sure we – as translators and human beings – do our best to remind people of the decisions in every text and their consequences. It might not be easily visible at first, but decisions are made – and somebody better take a good hard look at them if humanity wants to stay in charge of its international and global communications.

Addendum

Like numerous students before and after me, I embarked on the search for a topic for my diploma thesis with Michèle's, my supervisor's, advice in my ear: 'Get a life before you get a *Diplomarbeitsthema*' (sic). The sentence that was part of a presentation she showed us then was expressed in this mix of German and English. This invitation to really look and make out what I am truly interested in and what I wanted to find out more about guided not only my diploma thesis and the doctoral thesis I went on to write with Michèle. I also found myself applying this method in the Master's programme I pursued a while after having completed my dissertation and having worked in the field for about a decade. Also the topic of this contribution is, after my meticulously narrowing down and scrapping all that it is not, the essence of one of the things I am truly interested in at the moment.

Michèle taught me, and I am convinced many others, to let my curiosity guide me in my quest for a deeper understanding of things. And what is perhaps even more, by example and the way she encouraged me in my work as a student and later a faculty colleague at the University of Vienna's Centre for Translation Studies, she gave me the courage to have the confidence that my experiences as a human being matter in my research and also in other endeavours in and outside of academia. She is without a doubt the reason that I still believe that even in academia, which is all about clarity and hard facts and figures and proof and evidence (which are all good things!), there is a place for beauty. Beauty of expression and in other forms is never a waste because without the feeling that goes with the message, the message would simply not be complete.

Literature

Aragonés Lumeras, Maite & Way, Andy (2017). On the Complementarity between Human Translators and Machine Translation. *Hermes – Journal of Language and Communication in Business* 56, 21–42. https://doi.org/10.7146/hjlcb.v0i56.97200

BDÜ (2018, November 28). *Berufe mit Zukunft: Übersetzen und Dolmetschen in Zeiten des digitalen Wandels.* Press release, Bundesverband der Dolmetscher und Übersetzer. https://bdue.de/fuer-presse-medien/presseinformationen/pm-detail/berufe-mit-zukunft-uebersetzen-und-dolmetschen-in-zeiten-des-digitalen-wandels

Cadwell, Patrick; O'Brien, Sharon & Carlos Teixeira (2017). Resistance and Accommodation: Factors for the (non-)adoption of Machine Translation among Professional Translators. *Perspectives: Studies in Translation Theory and Practice* 26(3), 301–321. https://doi.org/10.1080/0907676X.2017.1337210

Castilho, Sheila; Morkens, Joss; Gaspari, Federico; Calixto, Iacer; Tinsley, John & Andy Way (2017). Is Neural Machine Translation the New State of the Art? *The Prague Bulletin of Mathematical Linguistics* 108, 109–120. https://doi.org/10.1515/pralin-2017-0013

Castilho, Sheila; Gaspari, Federico; Moorkens, Joss; Popovic, Maja & Antonio Toral (2019). Editors' Foreword to the Special Issue on Human Factors in Neural Machine Translation. *Machine Translation* 33(1–2), 1–7. https://doi.org/10.1007/s10590-019-09231-y

Cooke, Michèle [as Kaiser-Cooke, Michèle] (1993). *Machine Translation and the Human Factor: Knowledge and Decision-Making in the Translation Process.* PhD Dissertation, University of Vienna.

Forcada, Mikel L. (2017) Making Sense of Neural Machine Translation. *Translation Spaces* 6(2), 291–309. https://doi.org/10.1075/ts.6.2.06for

Hassan, Hany; Aue, Anthony; Chen, Chang; Chowdhary, Vishal; Clark, Jonathan; Federmann, Christian; Huang, Xuedong; et al. (2018) *Achieving Human Parity on Automatic Chinese to English News Translation.* 2nd revision. https://arxiv.org/abs/1803.05567v2

Johnson (2017, May 24). *Why Translators Have the Blues. A Profession under Pressure.* The Economist. https://www.economist.com/news/books-and-arts/21722609-profession-under-pressure-why-translators-have-blues

Kenny, Dorothy (2018). Sustaining Disruption. The Transition from Statistical to Neural Machine Translation. *Revista Tradumàtica. Tecnologies de la Traducció* 16, 59–70. https://doi.org/10.5565/rev/tradumatica.221

Moorkens, Joss (2017). Under Pressure: Translation in Times of Austerity. *Perspectives: Studies in Translation Theory and Practice* 27(3), 464–477. https://doi.org/10.1080/0907676X.2017.1285331

Moorkens, Joss (2018). What to Expect from Neural Machine Translation: A Practical In-Class Translation Evaluation Exercise. *The Translator and Interpreter Trainer* 12(4), 375–387. https://doi.org/10.1080/1750399X.2018.1501639

Moorkens, Joss & Dave Lewis (2019). Research Questions and a Proposal for the Future Governance of Translation Data. *The Journal of Specialised Translation* 32, 2–25.

Mulayim, Sedat & Lai, Miranda (2017). *Ethics for Police Translators and Interpreters*. Boca Raton: CRC Press, Taylor & Francis Group.

O'Thomas, Mark (2017). Humanum Ex Machina. Translation in the Post-Global, Posthuman World. *Target* 29(2), 284–300. https://doi.org/10.1075/target.29.2.05oth

Pedersen, Daniel (2014). Exploring the Concept of Transcreation-Transcreation as 'More than Translation'? *Cultus: The Intercultural Journal of Mediation and Communication* 7, 57–71.

Pym, Anthony (2013). Translation Skill-Sets in a Machine-Translation Age. *Meta: Journal des traducteurs = Translators' Journal* 58(3), 487–503. https://doi.org/10.7202/1025047ar

Pym, Anthony (2016). Getting It Right, Forever? Deconstructing a Professional Discourse on the Role of Translators. *Version 2.0*. http://usuaris.tinet.cat/apym/on-line/training/2016_getting_it_right_2.0.pdf

Ripplinger, Michaela (2014). *"There Has Been Some Kind of Explosion-Like Phenomenon": Press Conferences during the Fukushima Nuclear Crisis as Instances of Translation*. PhD Dissertation, University of Vienna. https://othes.univie.ac.at/35072

Ross, Alec (2016, January 29). *The Language Barrier Is About to Fall. Within 10 years, Earpieces will Whisper Nearly Simultaneous Translations–And Help Knit the World Closer Together*. The Wall Street Journal. https://www.wsj.com/articles/the-language-barrier-is-about-to-fall-1454077968

Sánchez-Gijón, Pilar; Moorkens, Joss & Way, Andy (2019). Post-Editing Neural Machine Translation versus Translation Memory Segments. *Machine Translation* 33(1–2), 31–59. https://doi.org/10.1007/s10590-019-09232-x

Setton, Robin & Dawrant, Andrew (2016). *Conference Interpreting. A Complete Course*. Amsterdam & Philadelphia: John Benjamins Publishing Company.

Toury, Gideon (1985). A Rationale for Descriptive Translation Studies. In Hermans, Theo (ed.), *The Manipulation of Literature: Studies in Literary Translation*. London & Sydney: Croom Helm, 16–41.

Toury, Gideon (1995). *Descriptive Translation Studies*. Amsterdam & Philadelphia: John Benjamins.

Vieira, Lucas Nunes (2018). Automation Anxiety and Translators. *Translation Studies*. https://doi.org/10.1080/14781700.2018.1543613

Aurelia Batlogg-Windhager

Human connection experts

The essential truths are somatic.
Pain, joy, love. We cannot escape them.
Our bodies tell us, whether we want them to or not,
what the truth is. Missing someone causes pain.
It causes pain because we love them.
Being with them creates joy, makes us joy-full.
This joy can only be felt.
It cannot be thought.
It cannot be pretended.

The Whole Truth
(Beyond Boxes on michelecooke.com)

Tea recommendation for this chapter:
Afternoon or Assam, with as little or as much milk or your favourite dairy-substitute drink as you like to go with biscuits, cake or scones.

About a year and a half after giving birth to my first child, our daughter Pia, I was standing in the kitchen on a quiet morning in early summer, ready to prepare a meal for the two of us. I can still feel the weight of the knife in my hand, my bare feet on the wooden floor, warmed by patches of sunlight that fell through the window. I don't *feel* it anymore, but I do remember very clearly an overwhelming sense of being the only human being on this planet. It had taken hold of me months before; desperation, a feeling of loneliness creeping out from every drawer I could possibly open in my kitchen – and my mind. I could *see* it was warm and sunny outside. Blue skies. Cherries in the tree. Pia giggling every time I played peek-a-boo while handling pans and pots. I *knew*, I told myself, that I was lucky to be there, at that very moment, at this particular time in history, safe and incredibly privileged compared to probably 90 per cent of all the people on this planet. Lucky to have a safe and warm home – and a heartbreakingly sweet, healthy baby girl on top. I *knew* everything was alright, even better than alright. But I couldn't feel it.

In hindsight – or from a psychological point of view – I was probably 'just' disconnected. Disconnected from my old life (we had moved from the capital to the countryside), disconnected from trusted old habits (I had become a full-time mother with no time to herself), disconnected from my own self (who was I after all these changes?). I could see the things around me, but they did not have meaning. No connection to my *self*. No context.

Things without context mean little to us, just like words without context have only little meaning. They don't touch our emotions as much as when we are attached to them through experiences and memories.

I recently went to my late grandmother's house, for the last time before it was to be torn down. In the kitchen cupboard, I found a small jug, the one my grandmother used to serve milk at breakfast or afternoon coffee. White and simple, old and chipped at the spout, it is not precious per se. But for me, it holds a lot of context, a lot of connection. In an instant, this little jug sent me down memory lane. Standing there, the kitchen smelling like it did when I was a child and Grandma still around, it made me think of sunny summer afternoons – many, many of them. Each Saturday, for as long as apricots or plums were in season, Grandma made apricot or plum cake – the best in the whole wide world if you asked me. And on Sundays, my parents would take my brother, sister and me to see her and have cake in her enchanted little garden. Grandma would put cushions in the garden chairs. Set the table, whip cream, make coffee. And we played in her garden, with her neighbour's cats if we could find them, and we ate cake and drank cold milk poured from the little white jug. I remember my mother being so happy and relaxed in her mum's garden, the garden of her own childhood. Looking back, she was so young then. She was my age today.

And then there were winter mornings before Christmas, when I was sometimes allowed to skip kindergarten and join my mum and grandma for early morning mass and then breakfast at Grandma's. Her driveway was covered in snow; we left footprints as we took the steps up to her front door. It was warm inside, and I felt so very special to be allowed to join these two grown-up women on what would otherwise have been an ordinary weekday. Grandma would light a candle and serve breakfast – bread rolls and butter and apricot jam and warm milk from that little white jug. It was all so simple, yet, in this context, just so, *so* unbelievably delicious. My brother and sister had to be in school, but I was here! Had any piece of bread, any cup of milk ever tasted better?

See how that little white jug is so much more than just that? Context adds worth and weight and sense and meaning. Context gives us feelings. The chance to make a connection. I love that feeling of being connected. I love context.

René Redzepi, the genius Nordic chef and founder of Noma Copenhagen, one of the world's best and definitely most forward-thinking restaurants, wrote a whole book about the role of time and place (i.e. context) in our culinary experiences[1]: A potato cannot be separated from the soil in which it was grown, he says. Once, Noma had a potato chip (crisp) on its menu, and it was served with dirt crumbs. The crisp was mostly just that – a fried thin slice of potato –, but the context, represented through the dirt, made it so much more than that; it connects us to the soil that has been around for thousands of years; to the farmers' knowledge and labour, to the sunshine, rain, time, patience and skill it took to grow the potato; the hundreds of steps that had to be made to bring it to the table where at this very moment in time people came together from all corners of the world to share a meal. Miracles!

Miracles happen all the time. People eat potatoes every day, but without thinking of the context(s), we miss out on opportunities to recognize the wonders that lie in even the most mundane of things. Neglecting context means missing out on opportunities to connect. Have I mentioned that I love context? It makes a simple white jug hold so much. It turns a potato into a reminder of our relation to and existence in time and space.

Also, connection to people and yes, even to things, makes us feel that we belong in this world. It makes us feel like we are *right* where we are. We (through science[2]) know today that feeling connected is a vital factor not only in people's happiness, but also in people's health – and that feeling disconnected increases mortality and is reflected in our nervous system just like 'real', i.e., physical pain. Loneliness, isolation, rejection – and other manifestations of that feeling of disconnection – not only disrupt our thinking abilities and willpower but also affect our immune systems, and can be as damaging as a bad diet or smoking. So my feeling lonely and incredibly sad on that morning in my kitchen was not unusual. I was disconnected.

Interestingly, theoretically, I should have known what makes us feel connected. Any translator should know that. Communication is what connects us. Seeing others and being seen. Understanding others and being understood. It really is that simple.

I believe that the reason why many translators, including me, chose our profession is that we want people to be heard and we want people to be understood.

---

1 René Redzepi (2006). *Time and Place in Nordic Cuisine*. Phaidon.
2 See, for example:
   Eisenberger, Naomi I. & Lieberman, Matthew D. (2004). Why rejection hurts: A common neural alarm system for physical and social pain. *Trends in Cognitive Sciences* 8, 294–300.
   Cacioppo, John T. & Patrick, William (2008). *Loneliness: Human Nature and the Need for Social Connection*. WW Norton & Co.

I know, at least, that this is true for me. To me, the mere thought of someone who needs to be heard going unnoticed is painful. Heartbreaking. I want to be there. I want to listen, and I want to make that person be heard, even if that means I have to translate their message for those who did not hear (or did not *want* to hear) it in the first place. Maybe – probably – I want this because there have been times in my life when *I* needed to be heard. I know how it feels to not be heard. Disconnected.

Of course, despite this underlying motivation for my being a translator, my average day as a translator does not consist of constant reaching out to the unheard and giving them a voice or platform. I am no activist, and I definitely am no hero. But when I look at why I still love translating, and why I can see myself being a translator for the rest of my life, I see that the reason is this wonderful feeling in my body, this absolute joy, this silent, inward satisfaction, this sensation of having done the right thing – when the words of my translation fall into place and I know: *This is it. This is how it is supposed to be.* Do you remember how it felt when you completed a tricky jigsaw puzzle as a child? Or managed to write down a complicated word? That's how I feel when I am happy with a translation I created. I feel happy with myself. I feel that things make sense. I feel that I am where I was meant to be. When I am able to serve as the missing link between source text and target text, I feel connected. I *am* the connection. This makes me feel in sync with the world. Or even the whole universe?

So, that morning in my kitchen with my little girl, I was not in sync. Too many changes (and a post-partum hormonal imbalance) had ripped me from my contexts. But then, the knife in my hand evoked an unexpected memory in me. About three years before this beautiful but sad and lonely morning, when I was still living (childfree, carefree) in Vienna, I was walking home after the movies. It was a warm summer night and it had just started to rain as I crossed the capital's marvellous *Ringstraße*. Warm drops of summer rain. I was quiet, lost in thought after the film I had just seen. 'How To Cook Your Life', directed by German filmmaker Doris Dörrie, follows Zen priest, chef, baker and author Edward Espe Brown as he prepares food and teaches his students how to combine the principles and concepts of Zen with seemingly mundane practices like cutting vegetables and cleaning up after a meal. Now, at that point in my life, having grown up in a small, thoroughly Catholic village in the Austrian Alps far away from the capital, and finally living the big-city life as a young student, I was neither a Buddhist nor intrigued by cooking or household chores in any way. But, as if by magic, this film had found me and connected with me on many levels.

When I was growing up, my family lived right next to my grandmother (the paternal one, not the one with the little white milk jug), a woman I loved immensely, and who I still, almost 20 years after her death, think of every day. She was born in the middle of WWI as the eleventh of thirteen children. Her mother, with warm, brown eyes like my Grandma, died in childbirth when my grandmother was three. It was the first, probably most devastating of many heartbreaks in my grandma's life. It was a very simple, humble life. She was never rich, never famous, never successful in a conventional way, never travelled the world, never stood in the limelight. Yet, I can only dream of one day being what she was to little me and to many, many other people. (When she passed away at eighty-four years old, there were several hundred people at her funeral.) Why? Because she did everything with love. Not the loud, look-at-me kind of love. It was the small, unimposing, everyday kind of love. The I'll-be-here-in-sickness-and-health kind of love. The warm, fuzzy, cozy, twinkle-in-your-eye kind of love. Just being around her made me feel safe and whole and so, *so* connected. When my grandma made tomato salad in the summer, she took her time without losing any. She always picked few but the best ingredients she could afford, and never threw anything out. She treated every knife and bowl with care, but also without being overly cautious. She appreciated every single tomato without ever talking about it. And she permeated everything with her calm, unwavering presence. This presence was completely unaffected by whoever was around her. She applied the same care to the preparation of a meal whether she was cooking just for herself or for others.

So, years later, when I sat in that beautiful old movie theatre in Vienna and watched a Californian Zen priest bake bread, it all felt familiar. The love, care, connection, gratitude, patience, grace, humility, mindfulness, respect, the finding meaning and purpose in the mundane – I had seen it all in my grandmother long before I even knew there were words for it. And so, without realizing, I connected with Edward on the big screen. Big time. It was so beautiful, so comforting to see all these qualities again, out there in the world, ready to be found again. But then I was also a little disappointed. In the film, we can see Edward lose his cool several times, we can see him get upset or tear up over seemingly small things. Wouldn't you expect someone who has been practising Zen for decades to be above such basic human reactions? You'd think someone who has learned from the greatest masters of Zen, someone who has lived in the sacred surroundings of a monastery for years and years would not be fazed by, say, people chatting in a cooking class or using kitchen sponges incorrectly. I remember thinking, 'If I end up crying over kitchen sponges after years of meditation, why would I even start to meditate?' After all, I knew very well I didn't need meditation to cry over kitchen sponges, figuratively speaking.

I did not know then that meditation is a means to connect us even deeper to all that surrounds us. Not being touched by things would mean to be disconnected – and Edward definitely wasn't disconnected. He was deeply in touch with and touched by his surroundings, animate and inanimate. There is this one scene towards the end of the film that, without my being aware of it, stuck in my mind for months and years, only to be released when I really needed to remember it. In this scene, Edward talks about what life sometimes feels like, how we all deal with what life has given and done to us, how the things that happen to us leave traces in our heart and soul, and lines on our faces. And then, he explains how on a particularly stressful and challenging day, it was the connection he felt to a teapot, of all things, that provided comfort:

> In the course of life, you get banged up, you get tarnished. So, in a way, it's like patina that we notice in teapots. That there's some quality about them that continues even though they're banged up and tarnished and stained and bruised. And people are not necessarily treating them very respectfully and carefully, just as, you know, us, we aren't always treating one another or aren't being treated respectfully and kindly and carefully, you know. And certainly, over the years, I haven't always been patient with people because I get in a hurry; I try to do more than is doable. So we were cooking in this very small space for, you know, a hundred people. [Edward pauses, and, remembering the particularly tough time he was having that day, tears well up in his eyes.] So somehow the thing that captured my attention on the kitchen walls, of all the things that were there, was these teapots sitting on the shelf. They had their place on the shelf, and those teapots especially, as I said before, they were more round, rounder than these teapots [shows teapot]. And there was something about them that was just plump and round and ample and bright and cheery. The shape of them, even though they were banged up. And they, they still seemed so willing, you know, to carry tea and water [laughs], and, you know, provide and serve the people who were using them. And so, I would look at those teapots, and I would think: If you can do it, I can do it, too. (Doris Dörrie, How to Cook Your Life, 1:19:23)

If you can do it, I can do it, too. This sentence popped up in my head as I was standing in the kitchen on said morning years later, feeling so banged up and bruised and tarnished and tired and hopeless, and so guilty for not being happy. I saw the cutting board with its cherry stains. Not perfect. Still doing its job, quietly, steadily, humbly. Wait. *If you can do it, I can do it, too.* And there it was – connection. To the knife I knew so well. To the imperfect carrots. To the old, imperfect pan. To my imperfect self. We were all in the same boat. If they could do it, I could do it, too. None of us were great or outstanding, but we were all doing our best. And that, on this morning, felt like enough. And so I let go. I let go of the fear, the urge to be stronger and happier and more perfect and less sad. We all are what we are, aren't we?

And so I started cooking. I started making meals for my little family and myself, and in the process, nourished myself back to life. I made connections with whatever landed on my cutting board – that was about as much as I could handle in the beginning. All I had to do was be there. Then, slowly, through showing up, through being present, knife in hand, I connected with my food, with our new kitchen, with our new home, with my role as a mother and primary carer, with my banged-up teapot soul. I added connections and context. I learned that just a bowl of simple pasta, prepared with love and courage and presence, can turn a shitty day around. I learned that a warm meal waiting for you at the end of the day sometimes says more than a thousand *I-love-yous*. I learned that feeding your body and soul wholesome, nourishing food will heal things you hadn't even realised needed healing. I also learned that sharing food is one of the most foolproof ways to make people feel connected. We feel seen when someone makes us food that we like. We feel loved when someone takes us in, hungry, weary, faulty as we are. For me, preparing simple, healthy, nourishing meals for others (and myself) is one of the ultimate forms of total acceptance. Of love. It says: *I see you. I am here. Let us share this meal.*

For me – on a good day – this is exactly how I feel when I sit down to translate. I guess that's one of the reasons why I'm still a translator and not (also) a cook. This, and because it's a much more peaceful existence. But back to translating: I address the text in front of me, written by someone who has to say something. *I am here*, I say, *I see you. I'm ready to hear what you want to say. Let's do this!* I wash the vegetables, heat a pan on the burner, glaze the carrots, chop the walnuts, set the table. I read the source text, look into the contexts, explore its purpose, consider my options, find my interpretation, my wording, my register. I let it simmer, pour it through a strainer, add it to another bowl. Now maybe herbs and lemon and salt and pepper? Done. Oh, how I love this process! Simple. Tricky. Exhilarating.

But then there is this: When we cook for someone, or when we translate for someone, we put ourselves out there. We make ourselves vulnerable. We dare to say, '*This is how I do it! This is how I like it!*' What if we are rejected? What if we fail? Embarrassment. Humiliation. Shame. Pain. Disconnection.

For me, when I was still at university, there was a lot of fear attached to being in class. When we were supposed to present our thoughts and translation ideas, I felt incredibly vulnerable. Today, I know why, and I am going to share my take on this, although that makes me feel vulnerable all over again. But here it is: I felt insecure and vulnerable because it is a very personal thing to open yourself up to a source text and let it run through your heart and mind and then turn it into a target text. Because there is something of myself in each of my translations. If you don't know me very well, you probably won't see it. But it is still in there, and something of who I am might shine through. Because every text needs to run through my brain and lungs and heart and veins before it enters my computer's keyboard through my fingers. Because as translators, just like chefs preparing dishes, we make decisions. We expose ourselves. We run the risk of making mistakes and exposing our ignorance and imperfections. We choose from words and phrases and registers and connotations and references just like a chef chooses from ingredients and textures and temperatures and timings and tools. We are guided by our knowledge (recipes), our experience (skills) and our intuition and creativity. You cannot *not* expose yourself when you create, when you make decisions.

It was hard for me to expose myself in that way for a long time. At university, so many students seemed so much more confident, so much more advanced in their knowledge and skill. Also, most lecturers seemed distant or disconnected from how I felt. No hero to identify with. To connect with. We heard, more than once and from more than one of our professors, that most of us wouldn't be able to make a living from this profession anyway. That 'computers' would take our jobs away. I felt as if there was no way for me to even hope I could be among the chosen few who would work and live as translators in the future, although I deeply loved everything involved in the process of translating from day one.

But sometimes, all it takes to make you feel like you can do it is one teapot. Or one person who sees you. One person to connect with you. One person leading by example. I was incredibly lucky to find that one person at university later in my studies. She was my professor, but, more than that, she was my teacher. She was living proof that flaws don't stand in the way of excellence. That being vulnerable – physically, emotionally – is a source of strength and power. Because it makes us human, and as humans, we connect. She held her head high in the face of adversity. She stayed true to her beliefs and values, sometimes in silence, sometimes outspokenly, and showed me how to stand tall against (real or imagined, inner or outer) Goliaths. She encouraged me to trust in my gut and to be daring – even, or particularly, in a conservative scholarly context. She saw me. I am sure she saw the flaws, but she also made me feel like there could be excellence. And suddenly, it all made sense. I finally felt like I belonged. If she could do it, then maybe I could do it, too.

And that's what it's all about. We can do it. Sometimes, we need someone to remind us. To see us. To hear our story, and to let us know their story through their actions and their words. I think, we, as translators, should be such people. We know how to do it, we know how to listen, to be there and to connect.

Human Connection Experts – that's what I call them, and that's what we should strive to be. I am incredibly lucky, for I have met several in my life. They made me breakfast and apricot cake and poured me milk from a little white jug. They hugged me and made me feel special on an ordinary day. They laughed with me through tears and believed in me, just like that. They showed me their contexts, their twinkles and flaws and shone their light on me. They heard me. Saw me, challenged me, taught me, changed me, inspired me, shaped me. And, at times, they saved me. Michèle, my teacher, my mentor, my friend, is one of them.

Grandma Grebi's summer cake

Line a 26 cm (10 inch) springform tin with baking paper and preheat oven to 175 °C (350 °F). In a medium bowl, cream 170 g (¾ cup) butter and 170 g (1½ cups) icing sugar for 10 minutes, using a hand mixer. Add 2 eggs, grated zest from 1 lemon as well as 170 g (1½ cups) flour and beat for another 5 minutes. Add 2 egg yolks and beat until combined. Transfer batter to the tin and cover with halved and pitted plums or apricots, cut side facing upwards. In a small bowl or cup, combine 3 tablespoons of (any kind of) sugar with 1 tablespoon of rum and put a little on top of each fruit. Roughly chop a handful of almonds or walnuts and sprinkle over cake. Bake for 45–50 minutes or until a skewer inserted in the centre comes out clean. Best served with whipped cream (and milk from a little white jug in a sunny garden).

Recipe based on 'Feiner Obstkuchen' (No. 1108) from Fanny Amann, *Meine Rezepte*, 1931. Translation kindly permitted by Hubert Krenn Verlag, Vienna.

Boka En

Categorisation and recognition:
Musings on misfitting and misunderstanding

Naming is not always an act of love.
It is also an act of tyranny, violence, and annihilation.
Putting things into words always means putting them into
some sort of box, fixing some sort of label on them.
The question is: How much space does the box have?
Is there room to breathe – or not?

The Lightning Flash. Language, longing and the facts of life.

Tea recommendation for this chapter:
Genmai, carefully prepared to reach just the amount of sweet- or bitterness that you enjoy.

Dear reader,

Thank you for coming. It's been too long.

I think we need to talk. About that which cannot be talked about yet cannot not be talked about either.

Don't worry, all will become un-/clear later / at some point / maybe never / how would I know.

But first, let me introduce to you the topic of this chapter:

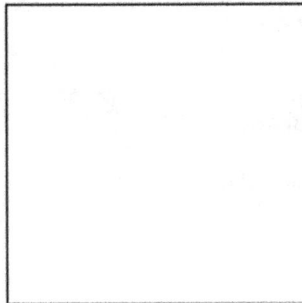

Fig. 1: A box (to make the world go round). / An empty space?

Fig. 2: A fig, too

Fig. 3: A date. Or even a number of dates. In any case, not a fig. What's the point?

Are you following?

Whom? What?

Why?

I think I need to take this more slowly.

Labelling things does something to them. Categorisation isn't innocent, and categorisation is all around us, from everyday acts of categorisation – *Is this avocado ripe? Can I safely hold my same-sex partner's hand in this street?* – to more formalised ones – *Our sample consisted of 23 women and 14 men. 12 of the women and 4 of the men had university education.* Both of these kinds of categorisation guide our actions: Whether or not we take that avocado depends on how we categorise it; how we analyse data depends on how we categorise it. At the same time, our actions guide categorisations: Categorisations are not set in stone or inscribed into the nature of things, but formed through acts of categorisation (Bowker & Star 1999; Foucault 2002).

However, it is not just others – things, people, actions, etc. – that *get* categorised *by us*, but also we who get categorised by others. It is not just *we* who do the categorising, but also *they* – if we want to categorise the world into these two groups, that is. And how we get / are / have been categorised also guides our actions: If we recognise ourselves as belonging to a certain category, this affects our actions. For example, we may adapt our behaviour to match expectations connected to these categorisations, or to contradict such expectations (Hacking 1986, 1995, 2007; Waidzunas 2011; see also Muñoz 1999). (This doesn't have to happen consciously. I'd rather let go of prioritising consciousness, for now and for later too.) And, of course, others' behaviours towards us will change based on how they have categorised us, and this will, in turn, affect our behaviours, thoughts, feelings, etc.

If I'm the avocado, whether or not you will eat me depends on your categorisation of me. If I'm a trans person, the degree and form of positive or negative consequences (social, psychological, and physical) that I may face will depend on people's categorisation of me, as well as their categorisation of transness more generally in terms of, e.g., good or bad. For example, people may categorise this elusive trans person (me?) as simply 'a man', just living his life, or perhaps a 'man' that's not quite a man, or maybe something/someone else completely. And they may then want to let me live that life that I'm living, or they may feel an urgent desire to show me what kind of life they think I should be living, and they may resort to physical and psychological violence to make their opinions heard.

Who am I?

Categorisation is also about recognition, and recognition is a tricky thing. If I categorise something as an avocado (and thus, as a millennial, intend to combine it with something else I have categorised as 'toast'), I *recognise* that that thing *belongs* to the category of 'avocados'. And similarly with trans people, or members of any marginalised (or not marginalised) group of people: If two people are categorised as a gay couple by the state, they are also *recognised* as such, and isn't recognition what we all are hoping for?[1] Don't we just want ourselves to be recognised? seen? understood?

Yes and no. Here is an example: Zhu (2018a, 2018b) did research on what could be categorised as follows: gay men and their wives in heterosexual marriages, where the wives don't know of their husbands' extramarital activities. These wives don't *recognise* their husbands' marginalised status, nor their 'sexual orientation'. Zhu argues that 'our' (whoever this imagined 'we' might be) view of that situation is influenced by two cultural norms: (a) that honesty is good (and, by extension, that dishonesty is bad), and (b) that sexual orientation (usually seen along the lines of straight vs. gay) is an important part of our identity. However, these norms are not self-evident.

I'm ambivalent about this argument. On the one hand, I can see the operation of norms around gender and sexuality and *truth* in how I myself think and feel about the argument, and I can see that these norms can, in principle, be questioned. On the other hand, I don't just want to let go of any notion of truth (and I do think that honesty can be very valuable in interpersonal relationships). And on the third hand, I do see how one's sexual orientation might not have to be the sort of personal essence that needs to be *recognised* by others. And then, on the fourth hand, there is a history of repression based on sexual orientation, and there are many people who'd much rather non-heterosexuals didn't exist, so taking a stand and showing that we do exist is a political act. On the fifth hand, gender and sexual categorisations are a legacy of particular, colonial ways of thinking (Lugones 2007). And on the sixth hand, recognition may well bring that which is recognised into being in the first place. (Clearly, I have more hands to play than I should recognisably have.) This is not a question about how 'we' see what 'is', but about how what 'is', and how we take part in 'issing'/enacting whatever it is that is (Barad 2007; Mol 1998).

1　See Browne (2011) for an instructive example of how such categorisations can be muddied waters.

Admittedly, quite often, such categorisation and recognition can be useful. If I categorise something as 'stairs', I know what to do with it, and because said object categorised as 'stairs' is usually standardised (in so far as the individual steps are all of equal height – indifferent and equal, one might say), I don't even have to do that thing that I do with it consciously, but can instead do it automatically. Sleepwalking up the stairway to heaven? Then again, this thing called stairs can also be an obstacle in one's navigating the world. A few years back, for a few months, I had knee issues that prevented me from climbing stairs effectively (as in, without a very significant amount of pain), so the object I recognised as 'stairs' was something to be avoided, or something that would make my access to certain walks of life more difficult. Wheelchair users face that problem too, more seriously and often over a longer period of time or permanently. Heaven does not seem a very accessible place.

Categorisation, or recognition, doesn't only take place in these individual moments that I've been talking about. We don't exist in a vacuum.

That reminds me: I should vacuum the living room now. I've been putting that off for days now. I'll be right back.

Okay, enough vacuuming. Let's get back on track.

Fig. 4: On track. When everything else gets blurry

Fig. 5: On rack. Lest things get blurry

Categorisations work performatively: They enact what they purport to describe. Categories are not ready-made entities but are enacted iteratively again and again (Butler 2011). They are not fixed and unchangeable but are remade all the time. However, while categories may not be fixed, they are not completely free either. Performativity draws on the force of historicity, and the above-mentioned iterations become 'sedimented' (Butler 2011). Categorisations also undergo such a process of sedimentation. This iterative re-cognition is not just an individual act, but one that a) even when we are thinking of an individual instance, is inextricably tied to a whole network of antecedents and descendants, and b) one that also happens in systemic ways beyond individual moments of recognition. Such categorisations also entail expectations. Coming back to my example with the stairs, Garland-Thomson (2011) invokes the idea of *misfitting* to talk about how ableist expectations (including their realisation in the built environment 'we' inhabit) interact with disabilities to produce exclusions: If one doesn't fit the mould (e.g., the mould that is stairs), one is excluded.

It seems (to me) that categorisation and recognition are tied up with power. Depending on the patterns of categorisation that have sedimented into you, this may or may not come as a surprise to you: You may think that surely, categorisation is power-neutral, or you may think that, of course, it isn't. For the sake of my argument, I'm going to assume the former: You don't believe me when I say that categorisation is tied up with power. (I'm sorry if you feel I'm not recognising you properly right now. We'll come back to that.) Where does that leave us? In this moment right now in which we're interacting with each other? In life? How do we talk to each other? How do we talk to each other when our basic categories of existence don't agree? How do we recognise each other when even the very thing we seek to recognise isn't the same for us? If we don't even *speak the same language*?

Miss Understanding

In academia (and beyond), we often like to believe that issues such as the one above can be solved by engaging in rational discussion and arguments. But that belief, too, is tied up with categorisations and recognitions and power. It goes back to the origins of modern Western scientific practice, during the Europe Enlightenment, when the 'modest witness' was the scientist par excellence, and said modest witness was imagined to be a wealthy gentleman (Haraway 1997). Wealthy enough to pursue disinterested science out of his (!) own pocket. White enough to be wealthy to have such pockets in the first place. What 'we' are doing (and it's fine if you think that you really shouldn't be considered part of this 'we') is a specific kind of knowledge-validation game. I call it a knowledge-validation *game* because (a) recognition also means that your knowledges and my knowledges can be linked to each other and validated against each other, and (b) that validation works according to rules (like a game), which aren't quite as universal as 'we' might make them out to be (Collins 1989). What do we do when 'not speaking the same language' means that our respective knowledge-validation games operate on incompatible rules? And how do we achieve understanding? And where might mis-understanding leave/lead us?

$$1 + 1 = 2$$
$$1 + 1 = 10$$
$$1 + 1 = <3$$

Fig. 6: Three ways of solving '1 + 1', according to different rules of knowledge validation; decimal, binary, and cheesy

Mis-understanding doesn't only have to with understanding, but also with ignorance. Thus, I would like to briefly talk about Figure 6 in relation to the issue of ignorance, which I consider in 10 (i.e., 'two') interconnected ways: ignorance of what's *in* these equations and ignorance of what's *outside* them. I'll start with the first one: The first way of solving '1 + 1' will probably seem fairly obvious to you: *eins und eins macht zwei.* The second way uses binary notation for the numbers, and variations of this equation can often be found on apparel marketed to self-styled nerds (insofar as they use said apparel to style themselves as nerds). It could also be represented as '01 + 01 = 10', but that would take out part of the joke. The binary notation uses only 0s and 1s, where a 1 means that the corresponding digit is 'active', with the digits representing increasing powers of 2, starting from the rightmost digit. So, translated to decimal, 01 means '$0 \times 2^1 + 1 \times 2^0$', which is 1. 10, on the other hand, is '$1 \times 2^1 + 0 \times 2^0$', thus 2. Finally, the third solution doesn't take the numbers literally, but assumes them to be stand-ins for individuals (sometimes called 'people'). And if you put two people together, you get ... 'love'. But while that understanding may seem obvious and commonsensical to some, it, too, is not as universal as it may appear, considering that various people have emphasised how romantic monogamy needn't be the norm (Barker & Langdridge 2010), or how love needn't be only or primarily about romance (Barker 2013). Being able to 'solve' these equations 'properly' depends on our *recognising* them properly, our not being ignorant of what's *in* them. For the first one, I need to recognise it as being based on the rules of addition using decimal numbers. For the second one, I need to recognise it as being based on the rules of addition using binary numbers. For the third one, I need to recognise it as being based on the rules of dyadic, monogamous, probably heterosexual (though in this case homodigital) attraction.

We might ask: What if I can't recognise these rules? What if I can't recognise the whole thing as consisting of Arabic digits in the first place? We might also ask: What if I *can*? Or: What if I *could* but don't want to? In answering these questions, we might, on the one hand, regard this I that doesn't recognise these things as a poor ignorant thing, and we might rejoice when we learn how to recognise the equation properly so we can solve it properly. Or we might invoke the mantra that categorisation is tied up with power, and then ask: What would *not* recognising these equations according to the rules that rule in our societies – or at least the one(s) that I live in – enable us to see? What other ways of seeing '1 + 1' might there be if we don't let ourselves be boxed in by the recognition that it *is* a decimal/binary/romantic equation? When I recognise the expression '1 + 1' to be based on a certain set of rules and solve it according to that set of rules, I call one potential reality into being, and, in doing so, exclude other realities, at least for this very moment.

$$1 + 1 =$$

Fig. 7: Space for your own notes

Clearly, not partaking in the hegemonic rules of recognition may have its advantages. (Black) feminist standpoint theorists have made arguments along those lines for several decades now (see e.g. Collins 2000; Haraway 1991), arguing that women, or Black women, can collectively see things that men, or white men, or white people, can't really see. A similar argument can be made about members of marginalised groups more broadly. The walls that box us in are invisible as long as we, ourselves, move within them because they are so normal. But when such boxes are used to exclude us, we run into them. A brick wall becomes very tangible when you run into it because it's been put in your way.[2]

Additionally, recognition depends on ignorance in an additional way. Ignorance not simply in the sense of 'not knowing' as a sort of accident that can easily be rectified, but as a concerted, structural effort to not know that which might undermine societal relations of power – an 'epistemology of ignorance' (Mills 1997; Sullivan & Tuana 2007; see also Sedgwick 1988). What if you, structurally speaking, just don't *want* to understand me (or I you, for that matter)? It's not just recognition that isn't innocent, but also non-recognition. How do we talk to each other when you don't agree with my basic existence? And how does our talking to each other create, but also erase existence, and the conditions under which different 'we's can exist?

Mis-understanding, then, can be understood in terms of mis-fitting, and mis-fitting not simply as an innocent condition that just happens to *be* that way, but as an activity, an enacting: Some of us get made to be mis-fit by the most

---

2   I take the metaphor of the brick wall from Ahmed's (2012) *On Being Included: Racism and Diversity in Institutional Life.*

powerful rules of recognition. They/we get made to mis-fit insofar as no space is made for them/us as well as insofar as space is made to be hostile to us/them (Puwar 2004). Ahmed (2014) invokes the metaphor of an armchair that has been moulded to fit the contours of our body and compares the comfort we experience in that armchair to heteronormativity:

> 'One fits, and by fitting, the surfaces of bodies disappear from view. The disappearance of the surface is instructive: in feelings of comfort, bodies extend into spaces, and spaces extend into bodies. The sinking feeling involves a seamless space, or a space where you can't see the 'stitches' between bodies. [...] Heteronormativity functions as a form of public comfort by allowing bodies to extend into spaces that have already taken their shape. Those spaces are lived as comfortable as they allow bodies to fit in; the surfaces of social space are already impressed upon by the shape of such bodies (like a chair that acquires its shape by the repetition of some bodies inhabiting it: we can almost see the shape of bodies as 'impressions' on the surface).' (Ahmed 2014:148)

And in addition to the exclusions enacted by understanding – fitting – and mis-understanding – mis-fitting –, recognition enacts upon us a pressure to fit. The mould excludes, and the mould moulds. If I get crowned Miss Understanding for being the best in understanding in line with the most powerful norms – *you understand this so beautifully!* –, where does that leave me?

The point

We have come quite far. Or not?

I'm not sure whether I have made myself understood.

And I'm not all that sure whether I *want* myself to be understood.

If understanding is so bound up with power and hierarchy and white supremacy and patriarchy and cisheteronormativity and ableism and classism and ... then what does it mean to want to be understood?

Am I supporting a set of interlocking systems of domination and oppression if I want to be understood? Because aren't these interlocking systems the very basis on which I can be understood in the first place? Does this make me a *bad person*?

How do I make a point when that point might be the *point* of a sword?

    a

    s

    word

    ?

Is solipsism the answer?

I don't think so. I don't want to think so. But at the same time, I am having difficulties grappling with the many contradictions inherent to shared categorisations, to mutual understanding. Perhaps my difficulties stem from my own deep desire to somehow categorise approaches to understanding along the lines of 'good' vs. 'bad' and 'right' vs. 'wrong'.

Perhaps, I've been trying to approach this problem in too abstract a way. Perhaps, an example is called for. So let me call on an example that has to do with how we do social research and how we use/develop categories in social research.[3] The example that I would like to talk about are demographic categories such as gender, race, etc. Quite often, such categories are deployed as unproblematic and obvious, in ways such as these:

> Women did participate in our online survey, but were outnumbered by men. (Dewaele, Cox, Van Den Berghe, & Vincke 2011:315)

> The participants are 25 Danes and Norwegians who have grown up in very different rainbow families. (Hanssen 2015:281)

It appears that these categories are entirely self-evident. However, such sentences make me wonder (when I let them, that is) how these researchers may have found out which categories to ascribe to their participants. And, indeed, there is a whole number of instruments that researchers use to do this. For example, there might be forms on which boxes can be ticked or empty lines can be filled in. Or they may simply have looked at their participants and decided that surely, they must be this or that. Or they may have asked. But the question remains: What would they have asked? What would the label for the box have said? Take these two alternative examples:

> Twenty-five participants self-identified as women, and 10 self-identified as men; all participants self-identified as heterosexual. (Harkness & Khaled 2014:592)

> In response to an open-ended question about nationality, nine participants self-identified as Qatari, seven as Palestinian, six as Pakistani, six as Jordanian, five as Sudanese, and two as Bahraini. [...] Thus, although most of our participants were not certified Qatari citizens, their status as lifelong or long-term residents gave them a sense of being culturally Qatari, and their attitudes and practices related to marriage reflected the country's way of life. (Harkness & Khaled 2014:592)

While in the first two examples, the categories seemed entirely self-evident (insofar as the conditions of their determination didn't warrant any sort of

---

3 This section is based on work I did for a Master's thesis that has been languishing in the shadows for several years now because I've been focused on other things.

elaboration[4]), these last two examples refer to self-identification as that which determines one's gender, sexuality, nationality. In other articles, reference is made to, for example, one's citizenship status or legal gender. We could also think of other commonly used characteristics such as age, class or dis-/ability, and again, we would come across a range of different ways of determining these.

There are a range of other categories too that get foregrounded in research. Among these, for example, may be questions of whether people are living alone or with others; whether they live in urban or rural areas; and whether they are single, in a relationship, or married. Again, one might imagine a range of different ways of ascertaining which category these people must have belonged to, and these different ways may sometimes give contradictory results. (Does one need to *identify* as 'single' in order to *be* single?) Additionally, different pieces of research emphasise different categories. For example, gender tends to be mentioned a lot; race can be glossed over, especially when there is an assumption that everyone is white anyway; living arrangements may or may not be made relevant; age often seems particularly pertinent.

And of course, this is not something that only happens in research, but also in life more generally. But why? Because we think the categories tell us something about the people so categorised, and through that, categorisations can help us make decisions, guide our lives. If we know a research participant's age, 'we' think, we magically gain a deeper understanding of whatever it is they said. If we know the gender of the person we're talking to, we magically gain a deeper understanding of who they are, along, perhaps, with an understanding of whether we consider them potential romantic/sexual partners (or maybe rivals, because jealousy is often enacted to be legitimate and even necessary in knowledge-validation games around intimate relationships).

Categorisations give us context, and context helps us make – or justify – our decisions. And of course, this link between categorisations and decisions can be immensely valuable, or even important. Whether I categorise an item in front of me as an avocado or a stone will affect how I interact with it. This will happen in combination with a number of other factors such as whether I like avocados, or whether I collect stones. And as someone who really likes to eat avocado maki, I'm quite happy that the people preparing them so far seemed to have relied on a categorisation scheme for avocado vs. stone that is compatible with mine.

---

4   See Latour and Woolgar (1986) for thoughts on how facts become facts by being stripped/relieved of context.

However, if categorisation guides our lives, we should ask which tracks we are following and how they have been laid, and who or what may be lying on them just ahead of us. We should ask which categories we make use of (and how they make use of us), which ones we maybe cling to, on what basis we make them, and why we believe them to be relevant. Our categorisations may not be accurate, or they may be pointless in the first place.

But what are we to do then? What *can* we do? We rely on categorisation so strongly both in academia and in everyday life that avoiding it seems impossible, and trying to do it differently is bound to lead to mis-understandings/mis-fits. In my PhD project, in which I trace boundary-making practices in LGBTIQ* activism and academia, I try to not assume certain categories, nor do I ask people about them in the interviews I do, instead focusing on how categories may or may not be invoked in the interviews themselves. However, this has been a difficult task, and one at which I am sure I will ultimately fail. In life more generally, I do often assign people to categories/boxes. I myself don't fit the usual rules of gender recognition, and this has led to many conflicts in institutional as well as private settings – from being spat at in public, to being denied an appropriate e-mail address by a member of the IT department at 'my' university, to torturing myself over the question of how much of a responsibility I have to act in a certain way in order to be recognised in a way that I am okay with. Failures abound. However, I believe that that doesn't mean I should just give up trying, nor does failing mean failing completely.[5]

Perhaps what I have tried in this chapter is one way of troubling categorisation, recognition, understanding: not pinning ourselves down to a single story[6] that we make ourselves believe we want to bring across. I have tried – and am still trying, not just here, but in life more generally – to be open to ambiguity and multiple meanings, perhaps contradictions (though this I am not very good at – or am I?). I try to seek out ways of understanding – including ways of understanding myself – that are not complete, comprehensive, rational and explicit, but partial (Haraway 1991), somatic, tentative, jocular, ridiculous. Even in doing this, I am caught in a profound ambivalence. I relish trying to derail my own trains of thought, and, simultaneously, long for clarity. And I try stepping outside the binary between ambiguity and clarity, recognising it as just another feeble

---

5   See also Halberstam 2011 for insights about how failure may not always be a bad thing.
6   The term is inspired by Adichie's TED talk 'The danger of a single story' (TED 2009), though it is used slightly differently here.

attempt at categorisation, contraindication, incantation. But/And I could play that game all day long and it would never/always bring me joy. There is no easy dis/solution. But perhaps, that is the point.

References

Ahmed, Sara (2012). *On Being Included: Racism and Diversity in Institutional Life*. Duke University Press.

Ahmed, Sara (2014). *The Cultural Politics of Emotion* (2nd ed.). Edinburgh: Edinburgh University Press.

Barad, Karen (2007). *Meeting the Universe Halfway: Quantum Physics and the Entanglement of Matter and Meaning*. Durham & London: Duke University Press.

Barker, Meg (2013). *Rewriting the Rules: An Integrative Guide to Love, Sex and Relationships*. London & New York: Routledge.

Barker, Meg & Langdridge, Darren (eds.) (2010). *Understanding Non-monogamies*. London: Routledge.

Bowker, Geoffrey C. & Star, Susan Leigh (1999). *Sorting Things Out: Classification and Its Consequences*. Cambridge, MA & London: The MIT Press.

Browne, Kath (2011). "By Partner We Mean …": Alternative Geographies of "Gay Marriage." *Sexualities* 14(1), 100–122. https://doi.org/10.1177/1363460710390568

Butler, Judith (2011). *Bodies that Matter*. London & New York: Routledge.

Collins, Patricia Hill (1989). The Social Construction of Black Feminist Thought. *Signs: Journal of Women in Culture, and Society* 14(4), 745–773.

Collins, Patricia Hill (2000). *Black Feminist Thought: Knowledge, Consciousness, and the Politics of Empowerment* (2nd ed.). London & New York: Routledge.

Dewaele, Alexis; Cox, Nele; Van Den Berghe, Wim & Vincke, John. (2011). Families of Choice? Exploring the Supportive Networks of Lesbians, Gay Men, and Bisexuals. *Journal of Applied Social Psychology* 41(2), 312–331. https://doi.org/10.1111/j.1559-1816.2010.00715.x

Foucault, Michel (2002). *The Order of Things*. Abingdon & New York: Routledge.

Garland-Thomson, Rosemarie (2011). Misfits: A Feminist Materialist Disability Concept. *Hypatia: A Journal of Feminist Philosophy* 26(3), 591–609. https://doi.org/10.1111/j.1527-2001.2011.01206.x

Hacking, Ian (1986). Making up People. In Heller, Thomas C.; Sosna, Morton & Wellbery, David E. (eds.), *Reconstructing Individualism: Autonomy,*

Individuality, and the Self in Western Thought. Stanford, CA: Stanford University Press, 222–236.

Hacking, Ian (1995). Looping Effects. In Sperber, Dan; Premack, David & Premack, Ann James (eds.), *Causal Cognition: A Multidisciplinary Approach*. Oxford, UK: Oxford University Press, 351–383.

Hacking, Ian (2007). Kinds of People: Moving Targets. *Proceedings of the British Academy* 151, 285–318.

Halberstam, Jack (2011). *The Queer Art of Failure*. Durham & London: Duke University Press.

Hanssen, Jorid Krane (2015). The Donor Figuration: A Progenitor, Father or Friend? How Young People in Planned Lesbian Families Negotiate with Their Donor. *Sexualities* 18(3), 276–296. https://doi.org/10.1177/1363460714532936

Haraway, Donna (1991). Situated Knowledges: The Science Question in Feminism and the Privilege of Partial Perspective. In Simians, Cyborgs, and Women: The Reinvention of Nature. London: Free Association Books, 183–201.

Haraway, Donna (1997). *Modest_Witness@Second_Millenium.FemaleMan©_Meets_OncoMouse™*. London & New York: Routledge.

Harkness, Geoff & Khaled, Rana (2014). Modern Traditionalism: Consanguineous Marriage in Qatar. *Journal of Marriage and Family* 76(3), 587–603. https://doi.org/10.1111/jomf.12106

Latour, Bruno & Woolgar, Steve (1986). *Laboratory Life: The Construction of Scientific Facts*. Princeton, NJ: Princeton University Press.

Lugones, María (2007). Heterosexualism and the Colonial/Modern Gender System. *Hypatia: A Journal of Feminist Philosophy* 22(1), 186–209. https://doi.org/10.2979/hyp.2007.22.1.186

Mills, Charles W. (1997). *The Racial Contract*. Ithaca & London: Cornell University Press.

Mol, Annemarie (1998). Ontological Politics. A Word and Some Questions. *Sociological Review* 46(5), 74–89.

Muñoz, José Esteban (1999). *Disidentifications: Queers of Color and the Performance of Politics*. Minneapolis & London: University of Minnesota Press.

Puwar, Nirmal (2004). *Space Invaders: Race, Gender and Bodies Out of Place*. Oxford, UK: Berg Publishers.

Sedgwick, Eve (1988). Privilege of Unknowing. *Genders* 1, 102–125.

Sullivan, Shannon & Tuana, Nancy (eds.). (2007). *Race and Epistemologies of Ignorance. Race and Epistemologies of Ignorance.* Albany: State University of New York Press.

TED (2009, 7 October). *The Danger of a Single Story | Chimamanda Ngozi Adichie.* [Video]. YouTube. https://www.youtube.com/watch?v=D9Ihs241zeg

Waidzunas, Tom (2011). Young, Gay, and Suicidal: Dynamic Nominalism and the Process of Defining a Social Problem with Statistics. *Science, Technology & Human Values* 37(2), 199–225. https://doi.org/10.1177/0162243911402363

Zhu, Jingshu (2018a). "We're Not Cheaters": Marriage and the Construction of Radical Honesty. *Graduate Journal of Social Science* 14(1), 57–78.

Zhu, Jingshu (2018b). 'Unqueer' Kinship? Critical Reflections on 'Marriage Fraud' in Mainland China. *Sexualities* 21(7), 1075–1091. https://doi.org/10.1177/1363460717719240

Rehana Mubarak-Aberer

Let's talk about *, baby:
Telling stories, telling realities

*The scientist, like the artist, works with a reality which he or she takes to be
true, and which others cannot – yet – see. [...] Both are cut off from 'the rest of
the world' by what they believe they know. Both are isolated by the structures in
which they work – the social, political, economic environment which shapes, if it
does not determine, what they see, what they understand, and what they seek to
express. And scientists, as well as artists, seek to be understood. [...] We all seek
to express the truth as we know it, and as we live it. Each of us has our own ivory
tower. And we would all like to let other people in, or perhaps to break out of it,
if only we knew how. [...] Tell it like it is? Re-arranging the facts is the defining
moment of human communication; it is how we let other people into our world.
It also defines the essence of translation: putting things in a different way. Science
and Surrealism – surely an incompatible pair? Depends on how you look at it.
Translation happens – if we want it to.*

Tell it like it is. Science, society and the ivory tower.

Tea recommendation for this chapter:
Double Mint, as hot as your lips will allow it.

I translate, therefore I am

When I was a child, I loved stories. One day, my mother took me with her to the
library. She got me a library card so I could borrow books. On that day, I fell in
love with libraries. I enjoyed standing in front of those huge book shelves with a
seemingly endless number of books – an endless number of *Realitäten*[1] – in this
very calm and peaceful surrounding. I loved the way the books smelled and to

---

1   The German concepts of *Realität* (plural: *Realitäten*) and *Wirklichkeit* (both of which
    could be translated to English as *reality*) are fundamental to the axioms of Constructive

imagine who might have read them before me. In all of these books were many stories that I could dive into. I think I spent at least half of my childhood reading, inventing little stories and drawing in the library.

But then, something changed.

I changed when I stopped diving into different *Realitäten* and started to look at my own *Realität*, which was shaped by the contradictions of different cultural values and identities and by the need to find my place in the world. I stopped reading stories for myself and started to only read things that I *had to read* for school, and later for university or for work. At that time, I was not aware of the connection between 'arts' and what I initially considered 'science' and 'translation' ...

And then, I met Michèle Cooke.

After my studies in International Technical Communication in Germany, I started to work in Austria and approached the University of Vienna with my idea to write my PhD thesis on politeness strategies in different varieties of English and the possibility to create a concept for an automated computational tool that helps raise users' awareness of commonalities and differences in politeness strategies used in different Englishes. And so it happened that I had the great pleasure to meet Michèle Cooke as my supervisor. Was it coincidence? I do not know, but I think it was a gift in two ways.

On the one hand, the discussions with Michèle and her evolutionary theory of translation[2] rounded off my understanding of (my) being a translator, of being

---

Realism. According to Constructive Realism, *Wirklichkeit* represents an objectively existing world. Humans and their environments are part of *Wirklichkeit*. *Wirklichkeit* is independent from humans' perception, while *Realitäten* represent (scientific/sociocultural/individual) constructions of *Wirklichkeit*. *Realitäten* depend on individual perception and interpretation (Wallner & Jandl 2006, 54–68).

2   According to the evolutionary translation theory, based on Darwin's theory of evolution, human beings – including translationally acting individuals – are considered a product of evolution, sharing cognitive and biological features that enable them to survive. In this context, '[t]ranslation as a human activity is an expression of positive cognitive abilities, of mental faculties which have been selected for because they confer on humans an adaptability which enhances their survival chances' (Cooke 2004:21). During the process of translation, human beings compare different *Realitäten*, identify the common denominator and transfer what is meant into the horizon of experience of the target text recipient. In other words, humans shift their perspective. All human beings are potentially able to shift their perspective and thus able to translate (Cooke 2007, 64–66).

a human being and of my understanding of 'science' and 'arts'. In addition, after reading 'The Lightning Flash – Language, longing and the facts of life' (Cooke, 2011) and 'Tell it like it is? Science, society and the ivory tower'(Cooke, 2012), I was inspired by the idea of re-considering and widening my perspective of translation as well as of critically thinking about the putative gap between science and arts.

On the other hand, as an absolutely reliable and wonderful mentor, Michèle supervised me until I finished my PhD project in the year of 2015. Throughout the whole project, she encouraged me to continue asking critical questions and to be aware of what I want to say in and with my work, to always keep my focus in mind while writing.

This was quite a challenge at the beginning, especially given that at my usual workplace where I produce, edit and translate technical texts at high speed for a variety of communication instruments, I usually do not write 'for myself'. So, Michèle one day suggested that – as a creative exercise – I hand-write seven sentences a day about anything and read them out loud to someone to check if they understood me. This was a wonderful exercise, which – together with the critical works of Michèle and her evolutionary theory of translation – brought me back to my 'roots' and reminded me of my original love for reading, writing and creating stories …

And then, my children were born.

Translation happens. Not only between adults.

> My brother, Jonathan, knew that I was going to die.
> How can things be so terrible, I asked. That some people
> have to die, when they're not even ten years old?
> I don't think it's that terrible, said Jonathan.
> I think you'll have a marvelous time.
>
> Astrid Lindgren, The Brothers Lionheart

When a child is born, we guess and try to understand its needs. The baby communicates its needs primarily by crying. As it becomes older, it uses additional non-verbal expressions. Often the primary caregiver understands the needs after a while. This is biologically necessary since the baby would not survive otherwise. At the beginning, food and physical proximity of the mother or another caregiver are of primary importance. The older the child becomes, the more complex and more variable is the meaning behind its expressions. The caregiver needs to translate all the time. It becomes easier when the child starts to learn its first words and later, its first sentences. But even if a child is at an age when they speak a language fluently, the need for translation remains. The child's innate curiosity and urge to understand the world leads to a lot of questions. Caregivers and teachers need to translate their perspective of the world to the child, taking into consideration children's cognitive as well as emotional capacities.

When I was pregnant with my second son, I expected my first son to ask questions – questions as to where the second child came from. I wanted to be able to react to his potential questions and I did not want to be speechless. Correspondingly, I collected children's books on basic sexual education, talked to him about this topic and answered his questions before he could even ask them. That's what I thought, at least.

When Christmas Eve approached – two months before his brother would be born – we went out for a walk one evening. My son was admiring the lights for a while. Then, he suddenly looked very sad. Without looking at me, he said, 'Do you know what makes me really, really sad? That one day we will have Christmas Eve and you will not be alive anymore. What happens with you after the last Christmas Eve that we will have celebrated together?'

At that time, I was not prepared for this question. At first, it *did* make me speechless.

Translating the world to a child is a great challenge when their questions deal with difficult topics such as death. We will all be confronted with the death of loved ones and with our own death one day. We all have different emotions and beliefs regarding death, and we all have different ways of mourning after a loss.

As caregivers and teachers, and considering the cognitive capacity of a child, we need to ask ourselves: Is it possible at all to translate aspects regarding death, loss or after-life and to ensure that the child does not consider these translations to be the only *Realität*? Even if we explicate the existence of multiple *Realitäten*, will the child be able to distinguish between different *Realitäten* and *Wirklichkeit*? If we raise a child's awareness of the existence of different *Realitäten*, would this awareness maybe overwhelm the child and decrease their future resilience[3] because they learned very early to relativize beliefs and values?

And then, I remembered the book 'The Brothers Lionheart' by Astrid Lindgren. As a child, I read it over and over again, and it was one of my favorites.

---

3   Here, resilience is understood as '[t]he capacity of a dynamic system to withstand or recover from significant challenges that threaten its stability, viability, or development' (Masten 2011:494).

This story tells the adventures of two brothers, Jonathan and Karl. Karl is terminally ill and will soon die. To make him less afraid of death, his older brother, Jonathan, tells him about a peaceful place called Nangijala, and explains that Karl will travel there after his death. But when Jonathan saves Karl in a fire, he dies himself first. Karl follows him to Nangijala shortly afterwards. There, they meet again. In Nangijala, the two brothers have many adventures together and help the inhabitants of that world defend themselves against the ruler Tengil. At the end of the story Jonathan is too weak to live on because of a weapon wound. Karl decides to travel with him to the land of Nangilima, which one reaches after death in Nangijala.

It was not necessarily the plot itself that remained in my mind and heart. The story also did not make me suddenly believe in a world like Nangijala or Nangilima. It did not impose any kind of belief onto me. Instead, the emotions and the open questions that were left after reading the book continued to live and mature in me. I understood the book differently at different ages, and so it accompanied me together with many other stories, helping me foster and build up my own resilience.

Communicating and translating aspects of death, loss and afterlife to our children is not easy. Sometimes translation can be done through stories, since they encourage us to shift our perspective and allow us to have insights into different *Realitäten*. These insights can help us construct our own *Realität*, explore the boundaries of our *Realitäten* and nurture our resilience without imposing and without excluding the existence of other *Realitäten*. Stories can help us cope with unexpected and difficult events in life. They affect our emotions, and it is our emotions based on which we act. This means that stories that leave powerful images and feelings in us can leave remaining traces that can help us and our children foster resilience by shifting our perspective and create real-world impact by shifting real-world norms.

In order to gain and train the ability to shift our perspective on a certain topic, it can be helpful to learn about the different facets of the topic. Although death itself as part of life is universal and affects all living creatures, including human beings, the ways we talk about, react to and cope with it can be influenced by many factors – such as, for example, our age, gender, sociocultural and religious/spiritual biographies, the geographical and political context we live in, our relationship to the dead person (or animal, plant …), our psychological state and general situation we live in, and the amount of support we receive and accept while mourning. The biography of the dead individual, their age and gender, the way why and how they die and how much time is given to be mentally prepared for their death play an important role, too. Losing a loved one due to death can

evoke many feelings in different phases – such as speechlessness, inner emptiness, resignation, fear, anger, guilt or hope. We all have our own way of coping
with this complex set of feelings and it would be too exhausting (particularly
in the communication with children) to explicate all these aspects in a purely
non-fictional text. To raise awareness of different possible varieties of dealing
with death and mourning, short stories written from different perspectives and
in various settings can help elucidate and understand different facets of loss and
mourning in different phases. They can be 'digested' more easily and – due to
their partial implicity – leave more room for personal interpretation and development without imposing.

Taking this into account and inspired by Michèle Cooke's work and evolutionary theory of translation, here, I am translating different possible realities of
loss, bereavement and mourning in the form of short stories[4].

I am more than grateful, dear Michèle, for the inspiration you have been
giving to me – not only in the scientific context and in Translation Studies, but
also in life. Therefore, I am very happy to have the opportunity to dedicate the
following stories to you. I wish you all the best of life for your future and deeply
thank you for being part of the story of my life.

Stories

> *Stories are important, the monster said.*
> *They can be more important than anything.*
> *If they carry the truth.*
>
> Patrick Ness, A Monster Calls

My brother and the goslings

On his fourth birthday, my brother stopped talking.

From that day on, he would only talk to the little goslings. Every morning,
he woke up much earlier than everybody else in the house. Nobody heard him
wake up and go out in the garden. Our neighbors had a few geese and goslings
in their garden. They had allowed my brother to come over whenever he liked
and watch them.

He even went out in the winter. He would carefully stroke the big geese and
take the little goslings into his hands, warming them.

---

4   These stories are *not* intended to comfort children or youngsters after a loss.

He spent hours with the goslings, whispering into their ears. Then he would hold them to his ear and listen to them.

He looked into their eyes. But when he approached our parents, our neighbors or other children, he would look through them. His blue eyes seemed to freeze so much that nobody dared to talk to him anymore, knowing – and maybe hoping – he would not answer anyway.

The goslings were not afraid of him or of what he had to tell them. When he approached their fence, they came to see him. Like an old friend.

Our parents were very worried about him. But they were also worried about themselves. They consulted doctors and psychologists who all told them to be patient.

Days, weeks and months passed. Nothing changed.

Then, it was spring again. And his fifth birthday approached.

Our parents had not invited anybody. Our mother baked a nut cake, my brother's favorite. Then, my father put five candles onto the cake and lit them. He said, 'Now, Jeremiah, you can blow the candles and make a wish. You do not have to tell us your wish.'

Jeremiah blew out the candles without saying anything. My mother knelt down and asked him: 'Shall we go out to the garden and celebrate with the geese?'

Jeremiah nodded. Our parents took the cake with him to the fence of the geese. They all came out to see Jeremiah. Our neighbor came, too, and wished Jeremiah well. She said, 'Happy birthday, Jeremiah.' Jeremiah did not answer. He climbed over the fence and entered the barn. For a few seconds, all geese became silent.

And then, something happened. An unbearable scream of pain escaped the barn. Our parents ran into the barn with the neighbor. Jeremiah sat there, holding a small gift box in his hand and crying loudly. The geese approached him and remained silent ...

Ever since he was born and ever since I could remember, Jeremiah loved the geese. The day before he turned four, I told him that I would hide a small gift for him outside. On his birthday, he woke up early in the morning to search for the gift. He searched and searched, but could not find it. Because he was interrupted.

Because he was interrupted.

Interrupted by the silence of the geese and the ear-piercing scream of mine.

On his fourth birthday, our neighbor was driving his car backwards from the garage. He did not see me and I did not see the car. I was looking for Jeremiah and am still doing so.

The pocket in the pocket

My mother used to live far away from here – very close to the river of the black dragon called Amur or Heilong Jiang. The winters there were cold – very cold. And yet, every day as a girl, mother walked through the taiga, which smelled so beautifully of resin.

She always wore thick gloves. Her grandfather had given them to her. She loved these gloves because they kept her fingers warm. But on a cold winter's day – it was particularly cold –, mother lost a glove. She didn't know where it was. She searched and searched for it. Her fingers became stiff and she cursed.

She ran deeper and deeper into the forest and it began to dawn. Mother got lost and became sad. She leaned against a tree and looked down. A warm tear wandered along her cheek – very slowly, because it was too cold for quick tears. But just before the tear drop dripped onto the snow, a golden cushion suddenly appeared underneath and caught it.

Mother wondered and looked up. 'Who are you?', she asked when she saw a big golden and strong being in front of her. 'I am the king of the taiga', replied the being in a calm voice and reached out his paw. Mother got a little scared. 'You don't need to be afraid. I give you my paw to warm your hands. Take it. It will make you strong.'

Mother handed him her stiff hand and closed her eyes. The paw enclosed her cold, fine hands and the voice said, 'Now, your hands are warm and your heart courageous. As brave as a bear's heart. When you now roar into the forest as loudly as you can, it will become quiet and nobody will come too close to you.'

When mother opened her eyes, the being was gone. But on her hand remained a pocket – a fine, warming detachable pocket. A year later, mother left Siberia. But she took her pocket with her on her long journey. She always had it with her. This pocket was always in her coat pocket. A pocket in the pocket.

In the years afterwards, mother still used to hike a lot in the forest and I accompanied her. When I got cold or scared, I put my hand in mother's pocket. It was always very soft and warm. Nobody else but me was allowed to do that. And whenever I did so, my voice became loud and firm. My heart became calm and, in my belly, there was a light. It was so bright; it shone everywhere – through my fingers, my nose, my ears, my toes. Then, I felt the bear's courage.

On a particularly cold winter morning, before mother set off to travel even further, she took the pocket out of her coat and gave it to me. She said, 'This is yours now – wherever your journey will take you. I do not need it anymore. There is already so much light in me – I am no longer afraid of anything. I am strong enough to travel alone now.' Then, she gave me a kiss.

Hannah and the halibut

Anyone who tried to see the fishing huts of Groeven Bay that morning was unsuccessful. It was so incredibly foggy. But as dense as the fog was, it could not withstand the tickling sound that came from Hannah sharpening her knife. It seemed as if the noise cut the fog into small slices at regular intervals.

Hannah had caught a beautiful halibut. She was looking forward to filleting it and selling it at the market. Such a beautiful halibut would certainly make a lot of money. And Hannah needed money very badly.

She urgently needed a wheelchair for her younger brother Hubert. Hubert was paralysed from the waist down and lived with Hannah in her little fishing hut. Since the death of their parents, Hannah had been caring for Hubert. When Hubert had been even younger, Hannah hadn't found it difficult to carry him. But now, he became heavier and heavier, and Hannah's strength diminished. In anticipation of how Hubert's eyes might shine when he would get a wheelchair, Hannah put her sharply sharpened knife to the halibut.

'Oh, Hannah, I'm so exhausted and it's so hot. Please let me go back home!', said the halibut, flinching slightly with his caudal fin.

Hannah frowned. 'But, halibut. I need you. If I let you go now, it will take even longer until I have enough money to buy my brother a wheelchair.'

'And if you don't let me go, my daughter won't have a father anymore', the halibut replied with his last ounce of strength. 'There aren't many of my kind left.'

Hannah was still doubtful. 'If I thought every day with every fish about how there aren't many of its species left, I could simply wait for my own death and that of my brother. I can't fish anything but fish.'

The halibut trembled a little. Then, he said quietly, 'It is not my intention to make you feel guilty. I understand you and know that you only do what you have to do to make your brother and you survive. But if you trust me and let me go, I promise that you will still survive.'

Hannah looked briefly out of the window, closed her eyes, opened them again, quickly fetched a small glass container, filled it with water and put the halibut inside. 'I'll bring you back home.'

Quickly, she ran to the beach. She felt her throat getting drier and drier. She knelt down on the shore and released the halibut.

'Thank you, Hannah. I'll never forget that', said the halibut.

Thoughtfully, Hannah strolled back into her hut. She was incredibly thirsty and took two glasses from the kitchen cupboard, filled them with water and went into the bedroom.

But when she saw Hubert, she was startled. He lay in bed with his eyes closed and sweating. She quickly brought him the water and he drank it in one go.

'Hannah, I have such a strong pain in my hip. I do not know this pain. I feel so hot and my whole body is so dry.'

'Let me look at it', Hannah said and raised the light summer blanket a little. Her breath fell silent. She didn't believe her eyes.

'What is it, Hannah? Why aren't you saying anything?'

'I must say goodbye to you, my dear brother. Fins were given to you. You don't need a wheelchair anymore. I will now carry you into the sea.'

With all her strength, she lifted Hubert into her arms and ran to the shore. Slowly, she put him into the water. Hubert timidly tried some first movements. It only took a short while until he could swim with his new fins.

'I will never be able to walk, won't I?'

'No, Hubert. But you will be able to swim into the depths of the ocean. To places I have never seen before.'

Hubert stretched out his whole body and felt a deep satisfaction and relief.

His movements with his fins became more and more flowing as he became one with the water. Hubert was happy about his new freedom and laughed. He turned a few rounds and swam back to the shore, laughing. Hannah stretched out her hand.

Hubert suddenly became serious. 'What do I do now, Hannah? Without you, all alone in the sea? Who will understand me like you, who will love me like you? What is the ocean worth if I have to be without you?'

Hannah tried to smile. It felt as if all the water of the ocean had dammed up behind her eyes. 'I know someone there. He will be your friend. I know that. Swim away – he'll find you. He has found you before. You will feel at home with him. And I – I will always wait for you on the shore.'

My grandpa and the half moon

A lasting memory that I have of my grandfather is his smile. I remember watching him sleep and watching the little hairs in his broad nose swing back and forth to the rhythm of his breath. When I felt like playing with him, I pressed a kiss on that nose. Then, he smiled with his eyes still closed. It seemed as if someone had turned on a switch in the night sky and a half moon had risen, because my grandfather, despite his old age, had an almost flawless, very dark skin – almost as dark as a night sky.

The very last time I saw this half moon rise, my grandfather was in hospital and I was already an adult. I hadn't seen him for many years after the riots.

The half moon suddenly jumped out of my grandfather's face, into my mouth and into my heart. The night sky became even darker, grandfather's hand unbearably silent in mine.

The half moon in my heart suddenly weighed heavily and sluggishly. What do I do with a half moon in my heart? When does it stop being heavy?

With these questions in mind, I was hiking to Kirigalpotta – for the first time in my life after all those years. Suddenly, I heard an unknown whispering voice. 'Veena, do you remember us?', I was asked. I looked around but could not find anyone except for my guide and my aunt, who accompanied me. I ignored the voices and climbed further uphill and felt a gentle wind on my left ear. I turned my head into the direction where the wind came from and could smell a familiar scent that fell like a drop of water onto the many pictures in my head and swirled my memories. It was the soothing and calming scent of jasmine flowers. I let my eyes wander a little into the distance and paused for a moment when I saw a group of jasmine flowers waving at me. They looked at me sadly and said, 'We know what is troubling your heart. It's his half moon, isn't it?' I nodded and asked how they knew. They replied, 'Without your half moon, you would not be able to see and talk to us.'

'Was Grandpa able to see you when he still wore the half moon?', I asked.

'Certainly, he did. Everyday he had to leave you, he asked us to take care of you. And every night before you went to sleep, he sent his moon to the mountains and asked him to bring jasmine flowers, so we could protect you. Do you remember the song?'

One of the flowers began to sing:

> Nila, Nila, Odi Vaa
> Nillaamal Odi Vaa
> Malai Mela Eri Vaa
> Malligai Poo Kondu Vaa

> நிலா நிலா ஓடி வா
> நில்லாமல் ஓடி வா
> மலை மீது ஏறி வா
> மல்லிகைப்பூ கொண்டு வா

> Moon, Moon, come running to me
> Don't stop while you are running
> Climb over the mountain and
> Bring a Jasmine Flower when you come to me

I remembered the song – it was a popular Tamil song sung to children. But I had not known what it meant when my grandfather had sung it.

'How were you able to protect me?', I asked the flowers.

'Do you remember Black July 1983, shortly after you were born?', they asked me.

'No, I don't remember.' I tried to remember, but not even fragments of a memory wanted to see me again.

'At that time, arson attacks were carried out on houses. Your grandfather was worried about you and asked us to look after you again and again. One night, when an arson attack was carried out in your grandfather's neighborhood and you were sleeping in the house, the moon came flying to us and asked for our help. We spread out our bushes and climbed from here to your grandfather's house and wrapped the whole house in a flash, so that for a short moment, it turned dark inside the house. Because it was so dark, you don't remember. But on the outside, the house was not dark, since we grew together so tightly that our blossoms reflected the moon light and dazzled all those who wanted to light the house on fire. We had kept our promise.'

I became quiet and humble for a while. Then, I sincerely thanked the jasmine flowers and asked, 'What am I doing now, with the half moon in my heart? I will never return here again, will I? Then how can I see you and talk to you?'

'We are not only here. We can be anywhere – you just have to look. Anyone who carries a half moon can see us. If you are lucky and keep your eyes open, you will find others who carry a half moon. Everything beautiful weighs heavily – and so does the half moon. But it is a gift that nobody can take away.'

Many years have passed since this hike and this strange encounter. The hike went on and on from town to town, from country to country. Now, I have arrived and live in a place where it smells exactly like in Kirigalpotta – especially when it rains. Today, when my family laughs, I see the half moon in them. And I smile back.

Merle's favorite color

When her mother died, Merle was still tiny. She was so tiny that her big toes fit through an Edam cheese hole. Per, Merle's father, swallowed when he learned of the death of his wife. And it seemed as if the swallow was falling into an infinitely deep stone well. One could imagine how it would reverberate when dropping into the shallow water in the well.

But the swallow never seemed to want to reverberate. While it was falling, Per heard from a dull distance how Merle called for his love. He caught the swallow with his last strength and looked up, where there were some rays of light to be seen that from time to time comforted the stones of the well.

And so it happened that Per began to concentrate completely on his daughter Merle and his work. When Merle was not attending school yet, her grandmother looked after her every day, while Per was working. When Per came home in the evening, he would play with Merle or read stories to her. Since red was Merle's favorite color, Per occasionally brought her something red: a red ball, red gloves, a red hair bow, and so on. Merle was always happy about these 'Reddies' and kept them safe. When Merle couldn't fall asleep in the evening although Per had just read a bedtime story to her, she would sneak into Per's bedroom on tiptoes. She would cuddle up next to him under the warm blanket and try not to wake him up. She would put her ear on his chest and listen to his heart, slowly rocking her to sleep.

Now, Merle was seventeen years old. Every morning at five o'clock, she got up to go to work. She worked for a large shoe store, where she and two other women had to clean the floor and stock the shelves before the first customers arrived.

Merle also cared for her father Per, who had become seriously ill. She lived with him in a small apartment. One day, Merle went to the baker's and bought some fresh bread for Per. When she arrived at her apartment, she greeted Per, who was sitting on the sofa in front of the television, as usual. Then, Merle went into the kitchen and cut the bread to size for him, covered it lovingly with cheese, and brought it to him. She sat next to him and handed him the bread plate. 'You must also eat something', Per mumbled as he took a slice. 'Don't worry, Papa. I have already eaten. What are you watching?', Merle asked curiously.

'Oh, I don't know', Per replied tiredly. Father and daughter remained silent for a while. 'Papa, because of the coming Christmas holidays, I have to work this afternoon as well. Would you like to lie down in the meantime? When I get home, I'll read something to you.' 'That's a nice idea. But you must eat more, my child', Per warned again.

After Per had eaten his slices of bread, Merle prepared herself for the afternoon shift and left the apartment. There was a big turmoil in the shoe shop. Bargains were hunted, one pair of shoes after the other was tried on. Merle tried to put back the shoes people had taken from the shelves as quickly as possible and to arrange the shoes according to size and product number. As she was stacking shoe boxes on top of each other, a box fell to the ground. The lid opened and Merle saw a pair of beautiful burgundy shoes inside. Full of admiration, Merle picked up the shoes and looked at them for a while. 'I would love to wear such pretty shoes', she thought. But she was startled by the high price on the label. Disheartened, she put the shoes back into the box and continued to work.

After her shift, she returned home exhausted. She did not greet her father so as not to wake him up. She got ready for bed and made tea for the two of them.

With two cups of tea in her hands, she quietly entered her father's bedroom. She placed the cups on the bedside table. She took his hands in hers and felt the coolness of his skin. 'Papa, I am home again. If you like, I'll get you the newspaper and read something to you. I made tea for us, too', she whispered into his ear.

He didn't answer, not even with one breath. Merle swallowed. It seemed as if Per's former heavy swallow, which he had always caught for Merle, now continued to fall in Merle. Merle put her ear on Per's chest, still warm, and listened for the beating of his heart. But it was quiet – there was nothing there anymore to lull her to sleep. A hot tear dripped from her heart, escaped the corner of her eye and slowly fell down her cheek. The tear wandered on and on, it was so strong that not even the bed cover could absorb it. Finally, it landed on the floor and stopped right by the bed. Merle, in her deep sorrow, watched this strange spectacle and saw that the tear – like a marble – reflected something red. Merle wondered where this reflection came from and examined the area around the bed – in vain. She lifted the bed cover to look under the bed. There, she saw a pair of beautiful wine-red shoes, carefully decorated with bows and ribbons. On the ribbons hung a small label with the inscription 'For my Merle'.

My father's garden

My father loved his garden.

Every evening, when he came home from work, he devoted his time to the garden. He looked closely at each plant, and it seemed as if he were talking to them and asking them how they were doing. He watered and cut and dug with great love and devotion.

When he learned that he was suffering from bone cancer, he did not tell us at first. He did not want to burden us; he wanted to spare us. Instead, he spoke with his plants – over and over again, until he realized himself that he was seriously ill.

Only then did he tell us. It was on an Easter Monday. He had hidden small gifts for us in the garden. We had come home for Easter, and we wanted to leave again in the evening, because we still had exams ahead of us at university.

My sister and I lived in a shared flat near the university and only came to visit our parents on holidays. They lived about 700 km away.

Although we had not been children anymore for a long time, it was tradition at home that our father hid Easter presents for all of us. Also for my mother.

Again and again, he would find new hiding places in the garden – that amazed us from year to year.

After about half an hour of searching, I found my present. Curious, I unpacked it and was amazed. It was a DVD – a DVD of 'The incredible Hulk', a series that my father and I used to watch together when I was still living at home.

'Do you remember, poppy sun?', my father asked me and smiled.

I nodded and hugged him. 'Thank you. That is a nice idea.'

'It's been a long time since we watched the series together. I remember so fondly the cosy evenings when we sat in front of the TV with chips and ice cream. You always ate ice cream and couldn't stand the rustling and cracking of the chips when I ate them. Actually, back then, you weren't allowed to watch TV during the day on weekdays. But mom and Sarah were always at music school at that time. It was always a little secret between us.'

My mother didn't seem to be overly surprised by this; she just grinned and laid the dining table. Sarah and I sat down at the table. Dad also sat down with us. Then he suddenly looked at us very seriously and said, quietly, 'I want to tell you something. I have bone cancer, and according to the doctors, my life expectancy is at most one year.'

These sentences still echo like a painful whip – after so many years.

My mother asked many questions and tried to find doctors and therapy options. Sarah even applied for a semester off so that she could spend more time with our parents. My mother took unpaid leave for all my father's chemotherapy. My mother and Sarah took care of him. They cared.

I, on the other hand, said nothing on that Easter Monday. I ate nothing and drank nothing. Everything the others spoke and did felt so distant, as if I had had headphones on. In the early afternoon, I got up, said goodbye quite wordlessly, and took the train back. I didn't want anyone to take me to the station. I wanted to be alone.

In my shared flat, I deposited my luggage and did everything as I always did when I came home from my parents. I put everything out of the backpack into the cupboards. I looked up what I should prepare for my studies in the coming week and texted my parents that I had arrived well at home.

At some point, I felt very tired. I took the DVD that my father had given me from my backpack and put it into the DVD player.

I did this every evening after my day at university. I didn't call my parents or my sister. I also saw my friends and fellow students only rarely – only if I had to. I also told them nothing about my father's situation. What would they have understood?

Every morning, I lay awake in bed for a while and stared at the ceiling. But not for too long, because I didn't want to start thinking. If only the smallest thought visited me, I locked the door and locked myself into my work. I worked a lot and my grades were excellent.

When my last exam in cell biology was imminent, I read through various documents for repetition. 'Do you know why Hulk has such a green skin color?', my father had asked me once. 'Because, like plants, he carries chloroplasts in his skin.' I briefly remembered the situation in which my father explained it. How he put a chip in his mouth with one hand and then operated the remote control with the same hand. I thought at the time that mom would certainly have been upset if she had seen that he had touched the remote control with his greasy fingers. And now she'd never be able to get upset about it again.

Enough memories – I thought – and turned that page of memory to continue with the exam preparation. I had to pass, and I wanted more than just pass. My days began with learning and ended with learning – only in the evening I allowed myself an episode of Hulk.

And then, it happened. One Friday evening, my mother called me. It was oppressively quiet on the phone. She didn't ask me how I was or how I was doing with my studies. She just said, 'Your father is not well. Sarah and I take turns with him. We need someone to take care of his garden. Can you come?'

At first, I hesitated because I still had so much work to do. But then, I gave myself a push.

It was just the garden – I'd be able to manage that.

And so, I packed my bags and took the tram to the train station. I took my books and documents with me to learn on the way. When I arrived at my parents' house in the evening, nobody was home yet. It was still bright and warm outside. I was very tired and lay on a deck chair in the garden for a while.

At some point, I felt a fly crawling on my forearm and scared it away. When I opened my eyes, I noticed the fig tree in the garden. It bore unusually many fruits. I went to the tree, took a fruit and bit into the juicy flesh.

My father and I had planted the fig tree together. My father had wanted to make me happy because he knew how much I loved figs. He had told me that even as a baby, I sucked on figs with my first teeth.

While eating the fig, I noticed how dry many of the plants in the garden were. And so I walked to the shed and fetched the garden hose to water the plants. But when I had connected the hose to the tap and turned it on, no water came. I tried it again and again, adjusted the connection – but it just did not work.

I began to sweat. I felt how my pulse began to race. How could it be that it didn't work now of all times? It had to work! I ran to the neighbor's house and rang the bell to ask for help. But nobody opened the door for me. Then, I had an idea. I looked for some buckets in the shed. I ran into the house to fill them with water. But when I was in the house and opened the tap in the bathroom, there was no water. Was the water turned off completely?

What would happen to all the plants if they dried up? It was my job to take care of them. I was getting hotter and hotter. My pulse became faster and faster and my throat drier and drier. I ran back to the garden and didn't see the garden hose I had left lying on the lawn. I stumbled and fell on the grass.

Nothing hurt, but I felt my muscles tremble and my clothes become tighter. My upper arms and thighs became bigger and bigger. First, my pants started to tear. Then, my shirt. I noticed that my otherwise rather untrained body became harder and harder and I was shocked to see my skin turning green.

I screamed and tore out all the plants that came between my fingers. I dug them all out and didn't care that my nails broke and my fingers started bleeding. Nothing hurt, I was just angry – incredibly angry. What good was it to take care of the garden when Dad wouldn't be there anymore? This garden would never be the same again. I shouted at the flowers and was frightened myself by the power of my voice. 'Why are you letting him die? Do something!'

I began to tear out the sunflowers and didn't let them speak at all. But one sunflower stood by the poppies. They suddenly stood up and protected the sunflower. 'Spare this one sunflower!', they said. 'Why should I?', I asked, reaching for the sunflower. 'Because, like you, it doesn't talk much. The other sunflowers talk a lot. When your father comes in the evening to give us water and to talk to us, the other sunflowers talk a lot about the day, complain about this or that and, sometimes, get really excited. But this one sunflower – it has never said much and has become even quieter. That is why your father planted it with us, because we are its mouthpiece and it does not sink in its silence. He never told you, but she reminds him of you. Because you speak little and never complain – let alone get angry.'

I suddenly felt very exhausted and tired. My strength dwindled and I noticed how my clothes began to hang on me. My upper arms and thighs were getting smaller and smaller. I looked around for a place to lie down. One deck chair was still intact. I lay down and closed my eyes.

Suddenly, I felt the touch of rough, cold skin on my shoulder. I opened my eyes and saw my father's hand. He was sitting next to me on a wheelchair. 'Well, my poppy sun. It is so good to see you again', he said in a soft, weak voice. My mother and Sarah stood behind him. 'I really wanted to see you and thank you for taking care of my garden', he continued. I hugged him and cried – long enough to water the whole garden.

'I am angry.
Angry that you won't be there anymore.
I am not angry with you, for it is not your fault.
But I am angry because my personal hero has less and less strength.
I prefer to remember you strong and green.
Not weak and thin.
I cannot bear that.
It is as if my strength faded with you.'

Several years have passed since my father died. Every other weekend, I come to my parents' house and take care of his garden. Every spring, I plant a new sun flower amidst the poppies. In his garden, I feel my father. And I miss him.

Hope

When the first real snow fell and it smelled of cinnamon and almonds everywhere, the children of Ringstorp built a huge snowman. He had a big head and three even bigger bellies, a carrot nose and eyes made of dark stones. The mouth consisted of a long, curved fir branch. He wore a red scarf and a blue cap. The children called him 'Elliot'.

Every day, Elliot watched the children play and enjoyed listening to their laughter. He felt very flattered whenever one of them proudly showed him to their parents.

One sunny and almost spring-like winter day, Elliot noticed a wonderful resinous scent near him. He tried with all his strength to look a little to the left and right and there – there, he noticed her.

How was it possible that he had not noticed her all those days? She was so beautiful in her green tender dress and her white soft cape that sparkled in the sunlight. She was not particularly tall – not much taller than him – but all the more graceful.

Intimidated by her grace, he at first did not dare to speak to her. But after a while, he gathered all his courage and said:

'Good morning, Madame.'

Being taller than Elliot, the lady did not see him at first. She looked around and then, finally, down. There, she spotted Elliot. Enchanted by this gentle man, she wove to him with her fir tree branches and shook off some layers of her snow white cape.

'Hello', she said, seemingly pleased. 'This is the first time in my long life that I have seen you around here. I am Hope. I am very happy to meet you.'

And so, Elliot and Hope made friends. Every day and every night they spent side by side. One cold night, when the sky was clear and the stars were twinkling quietly, Hope realized that her life with Elliot was so much more fun than it had been without him. She reached out her longest branch and gently stroked Elliot's head and asked, 'Isn't this a lovely night? It's a perfect night to marry. Don't you think? We can live our whole life together.'

Elliot was very touched and happy. But his happiness waned soon when he suddenly remembered the sun.

'My life will be much shorter than yours. When spring gets warmer, I will melt and not be there anymore. How can I give you such a life-long promise, when you will live all year long for many years – without me.' Hope pondered a while. Then, she said, 'I still want to be with you for as long as I can. Then I'll just be with you for one winter. It doesn't matter how long our life together is. What's important is that I am happy now and so are you. When spring comes, you will melt and your whole body will sink to the earth. The snow will become water and the water will vaporize into the sky. And at some point, you will return as part of a thousand little raindrops that make the wonderful spring flowers bloom. With every rain, I will think of you and wave to you, in memory of a beautiful winter.'

References

Cooke, Michèle [as Kaiser-Cooke, Michèle] (2004). *The Missing Link: Evolution, Reality and the Translation Paradigm*. Frankfurt am Main: Peter Lang.

Cooke, Michèle [as Kaiser-Cooke, Michèle] (2007). *Wissenschaft Translation Kommunikation*. Vienna: Facultas.

Cooke, Michèle (2011). *The Lightning Flash. Language, Longing and the Facts of Life*. Frankfurt am Main: Peter Lang.

Cooke, Michèle (ed.) (2012). *Tell It Like It Is. Science, Society and the Ivory Tower*. Frankfurt am Main: Peter Lang.

Lindgren, Astrid (1973). *The Brothers Lionheart*. Translated by Joan Tate. Oxford: Oxford University Press.

Masten, Ann S. (2011). Resilience in children threatened by extreme adversity: Frameworks for research, practice, and translational synergy. *Development and Psychopathology*, 23(2), 493–506.

Ness, Patrick (2013). *A Monster Calls*. Somerville, MA: Candlewick Press.

Wallner, Fritz G. & Jandl, Martin J. (2006). The importance of Constructive Realism for the Indigenous Psychologies approach. In Kim, Uichol; Yang, Kuo-Shu & Hwang, Kwang-Kuo (eds.), *Indigenous and Cultural Psychology. Understanding People in Context*. New York: Springer, 49–72.

Daniela Schlager

Trainslation and other movements: Some words about me and you

You say what
I hear
But cannot
Grasp
It's in my
Mind
My heart
Not out there
Somewhere
Else
Between us

(excerpt from) NoThing
(Beyond Boxes on michelecooke.com)

Tea recommendation for this chapter:
Darjeeling, but if ordered on an Austrian train, make sure you ask for the creamer of your choice or you will simply get it black.

When I was asked to contribute to this book, I was pretty stressed out. I was busy, didn't have much time and energy left and it seemed impossible to produce anything meaningful in time for the deadline.[1]

I probably wouldn't have tried if I hadn't learned some things from you. Like, for example, that meaningful texts don't have to follow academic conventions. Or that texts aren't even meaningful (or meaningless) per se. Or that it's fine if my English is not 'native' or 'perfect' or whatever other people might expect it to be. And, maybe most importantly, that such and similar convictions don't have to stay in my head only, but that I can dare to translate them into actions.

So here I am, freewriting in a small notebook while waiting for the *U-Bahn*. Not worrying if my text is going to be meaningful or good or whatever, not worrying, not even thinking much about it, just writing.

**

---

1   However: Thank you, Michael!

Change of scene. I'm not on the local *U-Bahn* anymore but on a train that is supraregional, international even.

I've always liked trains. I've often thought of taking a train somewhere just for the ride, without a specific destination.[2]

Trains are movement. Translation is movement, too.[3] There is always someone or something being moved, and there is always someone or something moving (transitively and intransitively, or is there even a difference?).[4]

'My' train is being moved by a bunch of people working for the Austrian railways. It's moving, through tunnels, hills, cities and a lot of non-cities, and it's moving me from Vienna to Salzburg (and if I didn't get off there, it would move me even further, to Germany). It is translating my home from one place to another for a weekend and then back again.

Both of these movements are back-translations: I grew up in one place, moved to another[5], and now I translate myself back (for a short period of time) and then back from there again (for a longer period of time). They're also retranslations: I do this several times a year, have done so for almost ten years now, and every time it is a little different. And they are self-translations: The someone and something being moved in this case are me and my home.

The train rides are also small parts of a big relay translation: With back- and retranslations for several years and several times a year, their relations get rather complex. Source and target are hard to determine[6], constantly switching places, getting blurry, melting into each other, becoming the same thing – a whole lot of pivots in a giant web. Not on this weekend, but on other weekends, the train ride

---

2   Without a *skopos*?

3   The online thesaurus *Thesaurus.plus* calls translation and movement 'related words' and says: 'Translation and movement are semantically related [...]. In some cases you can use "Translation" instead a noun "Movement".' As 'mutual synonyms', it lists moving, change, move, progress, passage, transfer, transport, transmission, evolution, variation, alteration, shift, conveyance, displacement, removal, transportation, transference, transition, and relocation. Nice, right? See Thesaurus.plus (2020). Translation and Movement. https://thesaurus.plus/related/movement/translation

4   What inspired me spontaneously to write this text was the train ride and the wordplay 'trainslation'. Another, more indirect source of inspiration might have been Michelle Woods' text on Tolstoy's translators, which uses the movement metaphor and includes trains in a supporting role – see Woods, Michelle (forthcoming). Traveling Translators: Women Moving Tolstoy. In Kaindl, Klaus; Kolb, Waltraud & Schlager, Daniela (eds.), *Literary Translator Studies*. Amsterdam/Philadelphia: John Benjamins.

5   Mostly by car, to be honest.

6   If not impossible – but sometimes, I like to think nothing is impossible.

is also a relay translation in itself: when I make a stopover somewhere along the way (at Lake Traunsee, for example) and then move on from there.

Oh, and all this is, of course, a long *Fortleben* of, among others, my *Heimat*.[7]

Trainslation. Moving back and forth and back again. Moving left and right and east and west and north and south and up and down. This almost sounds like dancing. Dancing is translation, too. Translating music and feelings (could these be synonyms in this context?) into bodily language, bodily movements, back and forth and left and right and up and down and vice versa and diagonally and in circles and so on and in ways much more complex than I, as a mostly non-dancer, can describe with the language available to me and printable in a book. These movements are a *Fortleben* of music, of feelings.[8]

I should dance a little more. The few times that I dance (without any kind of 'expertise' or the like), I don't worry. I don't worry if I can or can't do it, I just do it. And I feel free.

You are a dancer in many ways.

**

You move me.

You moved me in my BA years. You translated smaller into bigger horizons, borders into rainbows, potentially dry classes into flowers and boats. You translated questions into answers, answers into questions and questions into more questions – and all of it into aha moments. And you translated words into smiles.

Your translations moved me, not just because they were translations and translations always move someone or something, but also because your translations were often very unconventional (to put it in traditional discourse on translation and translators: you 'took many liberties'). And they were always 'better than the original'.[9]

---

7   Walter Benjamin and Steven Rendall (1997:155), one of the translators of Benjamin's seminal text 'Die Aufgabe des Übersetzers', describe the *Fortleben* ('continuing life') of a text in its translation as 'a transformation and renewal of a living thing, the original is changed'. See Rendall, Steven (1997). The Translator's Task, Walter Benjamin (Translation). *TTR – Traduction, Terminologie, Rédaction* 10(2), 151–165. https://doi.org/ 10.7202/037302ar

8   See also Haga, Egil (2008). *Correspondences Between Music and Body Movement*. PhD thesis, University of Oslo. https://urn.nb.no/URN:NBN:no-20848

9   For the record: I usually avoid constructing hierarchies between 'originals' and 'translations', maybe except for a few cover songs that I particularly (dis)like. I might not even believe in 'originals' in the first place.

Also, you moved me when you showed me how to twist and invited me to dance through the empty *Audimax*, to the sounds of *Twist and Shout*[10].

Sometimes, different movements go in different directions. Then, instead of our feet, the railroads twist. Trains make a detour and lose sight of each other. But luckily, sometimes the world is small enough that such detours don't last forever. Not all horizons have to be broad.

I'm in my PhD years now and you still move me.

You translate a PhD seminar into a space of time travel and other experiments. You move me back to a time where I found a lot of pleasure in writing and had no fear of being judged, a time before I unlearned to express myself. You move me to a future perfect (perfect future?) where I'll have unlearned the unlearning and will have found my voice. You translate the present to an alternate universe where it's very much possible to float in outer space and be down to/on earth at the same time. (Is this dancing?)[11]

You move me from ordinary (and sometimes dreary) tasks to something I unironically call 'homefun', to that feeling when you sit in front of the computer, smiling about your own work and being so focused that you forgot about the coffee you wanted to make two hours ago.

You move me from conventions to potentials, from the subjunctive to the indicative, from overthinking, self-consciousness and doubts (a submissive translatorial habitus?) to giving fewer fucks, daring, doing, having fun. You translate empowerment from a mostly empty and sometimes paternalistic word into something that actually feels like it. (I can do it. I'll just do it. It will be alright. I'm doing it right now!)

**

Academia (and not only academia) needs people like you. Thank you for showing me how to twist.

---

10 The Beatles (1963). Twist and Shout. *Please Please Me*, album by The Beatles. London: Parlophone. (The Beatles' version is one of many translations of this song. *Twist and Shout* has moved and been moved countless times.)

11 See also (to name just one song) Colour Haze (2017). Skydance. *In Her Garden*, album by Colour Haze. Munich: Elektrohasch. (Flowery music moving between grass roots and faraway galaxies that I often listen to when on a train.)

Also, you moved me when you showed me how to twist and invited me to dance through the empty *Audimax*, to the sounds of *Twist and Shout*[10].

Sometimes, different movements go in different directions. Then, instead of our feet, the railroads twist. Trains make a detour and lose sight of each other. But luckily, sometimes the world is small enough that such detours don't last forever. Not all horizons have to be broad.

I'm in my PhD years now and you still move me.

You translate a PhD seminar into a space of time travel and other experiments. You move me back to a time where I found a lot of pleasure in writing and had no fear of being judged, a time before I unlearned to express myself. You move me to a future perfect (perfect future?) where I'll have unlearned the unlearning and will have found my voice. You translate the present to an alternate universe where it's very much possible to float in outer space and be down to/on earth at the same time. (Is this dancing?)[11]

You move me from ordinary (and sometimes dreary) tasks to something I unironically call 'homefun', to that feeling when you sit in front of the computer, smiling about your own work and being so focused that you forgot about the coffee you wanted to make two hours ago.

You move me from conventions to potentials, from the subjunctive to the indicative, from overthinking, self-consciousness and doubts (a submissive translatorial habitus?) to giving fewer fucks, daring, doing, having fun. You translate empowerment from a mostly empty and sometimes paternalistic word into something that actually feels like it. (I can do it. I'll just do it. It will be alright. I'm doing it right now!)

**

Academia (and not only academia) needs people like you. Thank you for showing me how to twist.

---

10 The Beatles (1963). Twist and Shout. *Please Please Me*, album by The Beatles. London: Parlophone. (The Beatles' version is one of many translations of this song. *Twist and Shout* has moved and been moved countless times.)

11 See also (to name just one song) Colour Haze (2017). Skydance. *In Her Garden*, album by Colour Haze. Munich: Elektrohasch. (Flowery music moving between grass roots and faraway galaxies that I often listen to when on a train.)

is also a relay translation in itself: when I make a stopover somewhere along the way (at Lake Traunsee, for example) and then move on from there.

Oh, and all this is, of course, a long *Fortleben* of, among others, my *Heimat*.[7]

Trainslation. Moving back and forth and back again. Moving left and right and east and west and north and south and up and down. This almost sounds like dancing. Dancing is translation, too. Translating music and feelings (could these be synonyms in this context?) into bodily language, bodily movements, back and forth and left and right and up and down and vice versa and diagonally and in circles and so on and in ways much more complex than I, as a mostly non-dancer, can describe with the language available to me and printable in a book. These movements are a *Fortleben* of music, of feelings.[8]

I should dance a little more. The few times that I dance (without any kind of 'expertise' or the like), I don't worry. I don't worry if I can or can't do it, I just do it. And I feel free.

You are a dancer in many ways.

**

You move me.

You moved me in my BA years. You translated smaller into bigger horizons, borders into rainbows, potentially dry classes into flowers and boats. You translated questions into answers, answers into questions and questions into more questions – and all of it into aha moments. And you translated words into smiles.

Your translations moved me, not just because they were translations and translations always move someone or something, but also because your translations were often very unconventional (to put it in traditional discourse on translation and translators: you 'took many liberties'). And they were always 'better than the original'.[9]

---

7   Walter Benjamin and Steven Rendall (1997:155), one of the translators of Benjamin's seminal text 'Die Aufgabe des Übersetzers', describe the *Fortleben* ('continuing life') of a text in its translation as 'a transformation and renewal of a living thing, the original is changed'. See Rendall, Steven (1997). The Translator's Task, Walter Benjamin (Translation). *TTR – Traduction, Terminologie, Rédaction* 10(2), 151–165. https://doi.org/10.7202/037302ar

8   See also Haga, Egil (2008). *Correspondences Between Music and Body Movement*. PhD thesis, University of Oslo. https://urn.nb.no/URN:NBN:no-20848

9   For the record: I usually avoid constructing hierarchies between 'originals' and 'translations', maybe except for a few cover songs that I particularly (dis)like. I might not even believe in 'originals' in the first place.

Notes on figures

Cover

The images used for the cover of this book are based on art by Afishka on Shutterstock (https://www.shutterstock.com/g/Afishka/about).

Of bullet points and cows: Illuminating truths and truisms

The two slides of figure 1 and 2 were designed by Michael En. The photo used for the slide in figure 2 comes from Pexels on pixabay (https://pixabay.com/users/pexels-2286921). Figure 3 shows part of Winston Rowntree's 'Anomalies', a comic in the Viruscomix 'Subnormality' series (http://viruscomix.com/page567.html). A big thank you to Winston Rowntree for allowing his work to be used here.

The music in a name: Intersemiotic translation and musical cryptography

All musical notation was prepared by Benjamin Schmid unless indicated otherwise. Figure 1 shows 'Yachting' by Charles Martin; figure 2 shows 'Le Yachting' by Erik Satie – both were scanned by Michael En from Erik Satie's 'Twenty short pieces for piano (Sports et divertissements)' with illustrations by Charles Martin. Figure 3 shows a section from John Cage's 'Water Walk'. The scan is taken from Wikimedia Commons (version from 2 April 2018 by user Chrisfred3) and is licensed as CC BY-SA 4.0 (https://creativecommons.org/licenses/by-sa/4.0/deed). The QR code was made via QRCode Monkey (https://www.qrcode-monkey.com).

Categorisation and recognition: Musings on misfitting and misunderstanding

Figures 1, 6 and 7 were created by Boka En. All photos come from pixabay, with all edits to them made by Boka En.

- Figure 2: based on a photo by Jason Goh (https://pixabay.com/users/cegoh-94852)
- Figure 3: photo by SW Yang (https://pixabay.com/users/sweyang-1724813)
- Figure 4: based on a photo by Martin Winkler (https://pixabay.com/users/fotoworkshop4you-2995268)
- Figure 5: photo by Pexels (https://pixabay.com/users/pexels-2286921)

www.ingramcontent.com/pod-product-compliance
Lightning Source LLC
Chambersburg PA
CBHW070922150426
42812CB00049B/1359